Rick Warren's

Global

PEACE

Plan

vs.

Scriptural
Teachings on
Peace

James Sundquist

Printed in the United States of America

ISBN 1-933641-09-6

*"That very church which
the world likes best
is sure to be that which
God abhors."*

Charles Haddon Spurgeon
How Saints May Help the Devil
July 24, 1859

*"For what shall it profit a man,
if he shall gain the whole world,
and lose his own soul?"*

Jesus Christ
Mark 8:36

Contents

Dedicated to the churches of Jesus Christ our Saviour
in the 67 countries in which Rick Warren has tested
his pilot PEACE plan in 2005, the 131 countries[1] he
has been working on for the last two years,
to those who speak the 56 languages in which
Purpose Driven Life has already been translated,
and to rest of the nations throughout the
uttermost parts of the earth that he has targeted
to consummate the roll-out for his plan in 2006.
This is also dedicated to the tens of thousands of churches
which have already been stolen by Rick Warren's
teachings and to the saints who were purpose-driven
from those churches for opposing his teachings
and covenants, many of whom now have no church;
and to all of those pastors and church members
still on the fence about Rick Warren's teachings.
We hope this will help alert you to the magnitude
and scope of this religion and movement
and sound an alarm to those Christians
who have never heard of Rick Warren.

---

1   *Time* Global Health Summit Press Conference, November 1, 2005 —
www.time.com/time/2005/globalhealth/transcripts/110105warrenpc.pdf

Preface

To preface this book, I decided to begin with a letter I received from a church member of a Southern Baptist Church in Iuka, Mississippi. This letter illustrates the dissension and hatred the purpose-driven church movement is bringing in America and nations around the world. To purposely set brother against brother, children against parents, and the membership against the church leadership is one of the six things that God hates (Prov. 6:19). We should pray for those churches that are being torn apart by this cultic movement sweeping across the world.

—James Sundquist

Dear Mr. Sundquist,

I should have written weeks ago, but all my energy was directed to the problems at hand.

We cannot thank you enough for all the assistance — the prayers, the information, the support and the love. Nena Jones has been so faithful to relay that help to us.

Our story is not uncommon. The very first sermon our new pastor "preached" to IBC, flags went up in my mind as did my husband's and father's. I was raised to respect and support the pastor, and negative comments were not allowed. So, reactions were delayed.

As a 47–year member and the pianist at IBC for 33 years, I attended almost every Associational Meeting, many senior members group meetings, youth meetings, etc. Even before

I left my teaching position at a nearby community college, I volunteered for secretarial and cooking duties. So I was at the church a great deal of the time. Perhaps I was privileged to more information than most simply because I was present. This information led to concern and anxiety, but in no way equipped me for the terrible things to come.

In that first sermon, we were told, "It's going to be a rough ride; we may lose some along the way, but hang on," and that things would be changing drastically. My question was, "Why should we lose anyone?"

After months of personal agenda sermons, of personal confrontations, of witnessing many intentional attacks on others, and total disregard for biblical procedures, I realized this was much, much more than just a personality conflict.

His program was to divide and conquer—using his influence as pastor to create rifts between family/friends/believers. We now know his mission. We have a name for it.

I am the hot-head in the bunch. I am vocal and opinionated, so I tried to wait until I had definite proof. The pastor had laid his groundwork carefully. Even with proof, my complaints mostly fell on deaf ears. Once I found others were unhappy and we began conversing, we also began acquiring the information that other churches were struggling with what was called a movement. Then my friend Nena found verefication—it was PDC.

You entered the picture then.

I resigned my position as pianist April 8. I could no longer be a part of IBC. The difficult thing was not my resignation. What has hurt the most is the pure hatred on the faces of people in that Wednesday night business meeting. I thought they were my church family and friends—people I had known and loved 50 years. I could not conceive anyone would do what these people did to three fine, blameless men and their families, and then *rejoice.* I could not imagine others just sat back and let it happen. And some deacons (loosely applied) not only supported, but actually pushed this assassination. Even with proof that both pastors lied; even with proof the chairman of the deacons lied; even with proof our own by-laws were disregarded; our objections were ignored.

My heart is broken for my church. It is broken for these men and their families. Most of all, it is broken for those people who have fallen under the spell of these false prophets. I have heard from the pulpit on two separate occasions the words "mystic" and "mysticism." I have copy of the former head pastor's e-mail where it says, "click on your month of birth to receive your horoscope.

The battle has only begun. Perhaps God has plans for us to help others recognize, name, and oppose this garbage. I don't know. I just know He will reveal His will on His schedule.

It would be so wonderful to know you would continue to counsel and support us. You have been so invaluable.

Thank you again,
Londee Kent

Prologue

Spiritual Euthanasia

A Parable of Purpose-Driven Christianity . . .
A Way That Seems Right Unto Man, But Whose End Is Destruction

First they came for "resisters" and "pillars" of Brunswick Reformed Church, Brunswick, Ohio, because they opposed *The Purpose Driven Life* and *Church*. But I didn't speak up because I was not a member of the Reformed Church of American (RCA) denomination.

Then they came after a woman who was an elder lady in the faith who had been with the First Baptist Church of Dallas, Texas, since 1956, by shouting her down with spiritual euthanasia and aggressive, mean-spirited behavior . . . and the intimidation of seven attorneys, because she opposed them turning their landmark Criswell Center into a purpose-driven entertainment center. But I did not speak up because I was not a widow.

Then they held a trial for two families at Valley Baptist Church in Lakeland, Minnesota. But I didn't speak up because I was not a member of the General Baptist Convention.

Then they came after 165 members of Gardendale Baptist Church, Corpus Christi, Texas, and ran them out of the church. But I didn't speak up because I wasn't a Southern Baptist.

Then a brother finally did speak up and tried to warn Eugene Christian Fellowship because they had gone purpose-driven, but they threatened legal action and told him to stop spamming them. And I did not speak up for fear of being accused of spamming or being sued by a church.

Then a reporter for a large Christian radio network sounded the alarm of this clear and present danger. They ran the story, but received more gnashing of teeth from callers than they had ever had, so they censored this story from their print news service.

Then a brother on another Christian radio ministry broadcast testimonies of Christians thrown out of their churches across the country, but the network threatened to remove his show if another broadcast was ever made that said anything bad about Rick Warren. But I did not speak up because I had friends and family who were either employed by an organization that promoted or were in a purpose-driven church, and I did not want to lose those relationships.

Then they came after a large group of members at New Hope Church in Bend, Oregon. But I didn't speak up because I wasn't a member of the Evangelical Church denomination or the National Association of Evangelicals.

Then they came after a carpenter and his wife at Calvary Community Church in Phoenix, Arizona, with a sheriff to escort him off of the grounds, for trying to expose the deeds of darkness and the teachings of Rick Warren, telling the carpenter that if he returned, he would be arrested. And I didn't speak up because I wasn't a member of the Calvary Chapel denomination.

Then they came for me, and by that time there was no one left to speak up for me, because every church in the nation had become purpose-driven and part of his global PEACE plan.

— Compiled and Adapted by James Sundquist. Based on
Rev. Martin Neimoeller's poem written in 1945
© 2005 Rock Salt Publishing. Used by Permission

In Germany, the Nazis first came for the Communists,
and I didn't speak up because I wasn't a Communist.

Then they came for the Jews,
and I didn't speak up because I wasn't a Jew.

Then they came for the trade unionists,
but I didn't speak up because I wasn't a trade unionist.

Then they came for the Catholics,
but I didn't speak up because I was a Protestant.

Then they came for me,
and by that time there was no one left to speak for me.

(Rev. Martin Neimoeller, a German Lutheran pastor, was arrested by the Gestapo for opposing Hitler. He was sent to Dachau in 1938 and was freed by Allied forces in 1945.)

Introduction

The following commentary compares Rick Warren's global PEACE plan to scriptural teachings. The P in Warren's PEACE acronym stands for "Plant Churches"; the E for "Equip Leaders"; the A for "Assist the Poor"; the C for "Care for the Sick"; and the E for "Educate the Next Generation." Who can be against this? Well, we shall soon see. Warren announced his global PEACE plan on April 17, 2005, at Angel Stadium in Anaheim, California, to an audience of 30,000 people during a church service marking the twenty-fifth anniversary of Saddleback Church. Earlier in 2005, Warren had previewed it when he disclosed on CNN's "Larry King Live":

> And we're right now doing a test pilot of the PEACE plan in 67 countries. We're about a year and a half into it. It's a two-year test plan. We plan to go public with it—well, now, it's going public on "Larry King"—but **we plan to go public with it in 2006, which is to mobilize hundreds of thousands of small groups that have done the 40 days of purpose in churches and communities** and civic groups and corporations—**churches that have done 40 days of purpose in groups to do these five things around the world.** And that's really why I was in Rwanda, Uganda and Kenya, to test that."[2]

---

2   http://transcripts.cnn.com/TRANSCRIPTS/0503/22/lkl.01.html

Chapter 1

Opening Song at Rick Warren's Global PEACE Plan Inauguration

Purple Haze

Rick Warren launched his global PEACE plan on April 17, 2005, during Saddleback Church's twenty-fifth anniversary celebration. During the unveiling he sang "Purple Haze," written by Jimi Hendrix about LSD, a psychedelic drug, and demonic visions. Here are the lyrics:

> Purple haze all in my brain
> Lately things just don't seem the same
> Actin' funny, but I don't know why
> 'Scuse me while I kiss the sky
> Purple haze all around
> Don't know if I'm comin' up or down
> Am I happy or in misery?
> Whatever it is that girl put a spell on me
> Purple haze all in my eyes
> Don't know if it's day or night
> You got me blowin', blowin' my mind
> Is it tomorrow, or just the end of time?[3]

---

3   © 1967 by Jimi Hendrix — www.songfacts.com/lyrics.php?findsong=2553

David Cloud's research about Jimi Hendrix reveals that music was Jimi Hendrix' god. Apparently Hendrix attended church some in his youth, because he later testified: "I used to go to Sunday School **but the only thing I believe in now is music."**[4]

Is this the example Rick Warren wants to set in leading his sober and vigilant billion-man Christian army? Even if Rick Warren sang "Purple Haze" in jest to inaugurate his global PEACE plan, it still has the appearance of evil and is a bad witness for a Christian. Rick Warren's justification for defending the singing of "Purple Haze" before his congregation is like saying, "Well, I did a séance with all of my friends just for the fun of it and to help set the tone and stage for the New Reformation." What a song to pick; one whose author regularly took LSD and promoted a psychedelic culture!

It is astonishing that Rick Warren would choose a song which glorifies drugs used to produce magical effects. This is not the way to attain either personal perfect peace or the global peace that Jesus Christ Himself will usher in with the millennium.

It was commonly known to all of us who grew up in the sixties that this song was identified with LSD. This song should be a red flag for any Christian that grew up then. But for the children of the children of the sixties who do not know to what the song was originally referring, it is a clear stumbling block and brings to mind the following scriptural warning: "And whosoever shall offend one of these little ones that believe in me, it is better for him that a millstone were hanged about his neck, and he were cast into the sea."[5] (For more on Jimi Hendrix, see Appendix C.)

Promoting a song which glorifies evil and/or is well known and identified with the drug culture, and the fact that he has not publicly repented for it, should disqualify Warren from being a

---

4   Hendrix, cited by Curtis Knight, *Jimi*

5   Mark 9:42

pastor at all, let alone "America's Pastor" — the title *Time* maga-zine bestowed upon him:

> When *Time* magazine comes out and calls me, quote, "America's pastor," I can't tell you what that does in my life because it's something that I really didn't want. And some people say, "How could he be America's pastor when we're not all Christians?" Well, I can't, okay? You know, somebody has got to be America's rabbi, somebody has got to be America's imam, right? But if that is a role that I'm going to play for one segment of our society, then I want to represent them and the things they value — humility, integrity and generosity — with intelligence and integrity. Those are the three important values to me.[6]

If Rick Warren actually accepts the mantle of "America's pastor," he should be held to an even stricter accounting as an elder of elders. In actuality, there is no such biblical mandate for any single man having the authority to be any nation's pastor. *Nobody* needs to be "America's pastor" . . . and nobody should be![7]

Now, Rick Warren seems to have assumed upon himself the role of the world's pastor, or as he puts it, the leader of a billion-man Christian army. Didn't the First Reformation teach us anything? Have we forgotten what Lord Acton said: "Power tends to corrupt and absolute power corrupts absolutely"?[8] Not even the apostles Paul or Peter possessed final authority over the whole early church. In fact, they taught against it! For an in-depth study of why the Bible does not support the absolute sovereignty of a single pastor in a church, see: "Pastor Is Master, Isn't He?"[9]

6 www.pewforum.org/events/index.php?EventID=80

7 See article entitled "Pastor Is Master, Isn't He?, which demonstrates that Jesus is our ultimate Shepherd/Pastor.

8 www.phrases.org.uk/meanings/288200.html

9 www.rock-to-salt.cephasministry.com/pastor_1.html

Music, particularly in the context of a church service, needs to conform to the following scriptural criteria — qualities completely lacking in "Purple Haze."

> Finally, brethren, whatsoever things are true, whatsoever things are honest, whatsoever things are just, whatsoever things are pure, whatsoever things are lovely, whatsoever things are of good report; if there be any virtue, and if there be any praise, think on these things.[10]

The scriptural criteria found in Philippians, to be sure, is exactly what we find in the kind of song Jesus Christ has in mind for *His global peace plan*:

> And they sing the song of Moses the servant of God, and the **song of the Lamb,** saying, Great and marvellous are thy works, Lord God Almighty; just and true are thy ways, thou King of saints.[11]

> And **they sung a new song**, saying, Thou art worthy to take the book, and to open the seals thereof: for thou wast slain, and hast redeemed us to God by thy blood out of every kindred, and tongue, and people, and nation.[12]

> And **they sung as it were a new song before the throne,** and before the four beasts, and the elders: and no man could learn that song but the hundred and forty and four thousand, which were redeemed from the earth.[13]

---

10 Philippians 4:8

11 Revelation 15:3

12 Revelation 5:9

13 Revelation 14:3

Chapter 2

What Is Missing?

Holy Spirit

What is startling about Warren's PEACE plan is not so much what it contains, but what it does *not* contain. There is *no* mention of our adversary in spiritual warfare. There is *no* mention of the Holy Spirit in his global PEACE plan. Bob DeWaay exposes this fatal flaw in his new book, *Redefining Christianity,* in the chapter entitled "Understanding the Purpose-Driven Movement."[14]

Where is the prince of the power of the air from scripture, which any biblical peace plan must take into account? "Wherein in time past ye walked according to the course of this world, according to the prince of the power of the air, the spirit that now worketh in the children of disobedience."[15]

Satan still has temporary possession of the kingdoms of this earth; he offered them to Jesus as a temptation in the wilderness at the Lord's first coming. In fact, Satan will usher in a global peace with signs and wonders that will appear to defeat the giants of Rick Warren's PEACE plan. "For we wrestle not against flesh and blood, but against principalities, against powers, against the rulers of the darkness of this world, against spiritual wickedness in high places."[16]

---

14 21st Century Press, © 2006

15 Ephesians 2:2.

16 Ephesians 6:12

Warren's plan implies we can simply restore the earth to its Garden of Eden status before Christ returns, but no temporal worldwide peace plan can ultimately succeed until these principalities are conquered and defeated. This will be done by Jesus Christ Himself on the Day of the Lord, when His enemies will be destroyed at the brightness of His second coming. Where are the principalities in Rick Warren's peace plan? Where is the war? When has the strong man been bound for good? "Or else how can one enter into a strong man's house, and spoil his goods, except he first bind the strong man? and then he will spoil his house."[17]

Fear of the Lord

It it not surprising that there are no published statements by Rick Warren mentioning the fear of the Lord in his global PEACE plan, because he does not teach it in his *Purpose Driven Life* book, the trunk from which the branch of his global PEACE plan grew. In fact, he teaches the opposite: "We give ourselves to him, **not out of fear or duty**, but in love."[18]

He later states: "We obey God, **not out of duty or fear** or compulsion, but because we love him and trust that he knows what is best for us."[19]

And a third time: "**We don't serve God out of guilt or fear** or even duty, but out of joy, and deep gratitude for what he's done for us."[20]

Warren also quotes Psalm 147:11 from the CEV: "The Lord is pleased only with those who worship him and trust his love."[21]

---

17 Matthew 12:29

18 *The Purpose Driven Life* (Zondervan Publishing, 2005), p. 77

19 Ibid., p. 95

20 Ibid., p. 228

21 Ibid., p. 64

In the spirit of omission so prevalent in Warren's publications, this mangled translation takes away the most important qualifier — the most important phrase — **"for those who fear him."**

"The LORD **taketh pleasure in them that fear him,** in those that hope in his mercy."[22] According to *Strong's Lexicon*, the Hebrew word for "fear" is *yare* which means reverence and fear.

But of course we obey and give ourselves to Him out of the fear of the Lord. For more documentation on the fear of the Lord, see the article "Fear of the Lord"[23] and chapter three of *Who's Driving the Purpose Driven Church?*[24]

Scripture says much about fearing the Lord:

The fear of the LORD is the beginning of wisdom: and the knowledge of the holy is understanding.[25]

There is no fear of God before their eyes.[26]

According to *Strong's Lexicon*, the Greek for "fear" here is *phobos*, which means "fear, dread, terror, reverence."

. . . Let us have grace, whereby we may serve God acceptably with reverence and godly fear: For our God is a consuming fire. [27]

Without this critical ingredient, Rick Warren's PEACE plan does not have a legitimate beginning or foundation. There is no

---

22   Psalm 147:11

23   Rock Salt Publishing

24   Bible Belt Publishing, Oklahoma City, 2004

25   Proverbs 9:10

26   Romans 3:18

27   Hebrews 12:28–29

expiration date on the fear of the Lord (it will be present even during the millennium, Jesus Christ's global peace plan on earth). Any true peace plan for the earth must contain this pillar. The Antichrist's peace platform certainly won't contain it. At the end of the age, an angel from Heaven affirms that fearing the Lord is an everlasting command, which therefore must extend it through the millennium: "And I saw another angel fly in the midst of heaven, having the **everlasting gospel** to preach unto them that dwell on the earth, and to every nation, and kindred, and tongue, and people, Saying with a loud voice, **Fear God, and give glory to him. . . ."**[28]

Blood of Jesus

Rick Warren quotes 2 Corinthians 5:18–19 (although he doesn't cite the translation, it is from the CEV): "God sent Christ to make peace between himself and us."[29]

A sound and complete version of these verses will say:

> And all things are of God, who hath **reconciled** us to himself by Jesus Christ, and hath given to us the ministry of **reconciliation**; To wit, that God was in Christ, **reconciling the world unto himself**, not imputing their trespasses unto them; and hath committed unto us the word of reconciliation.[30]

Reconciling all mankind to God requires exclusively the applied shed blood of Jesus Christ. As that discerning old lady in the old hamburger commercial asked 'Where's the beef?', we need to be asking of Warren's global PEACE plan: "Where's the 'blood' (of Jesus)?" "And almost all things are by the law purged with

28 Revelation 14:6–7

29 Warren Smith, *Deceived on Purpose* (Conscience Press, 2004), p. 127

30 2 Corinthians 5:18–19, KJV

blood; and without shedding of blood there is no remission [forgiveness]."[31]

Godly Peace

Rick Warren's global PEACE plan is peace as the world knows it. The world loves his PEACE plan because it prescribes a peaceful kingdom now for the earth rather than "thy kingdom come" (when Christ returns). Warren seeks to prepare a place for us that where we are, Jesus may be also. **But Jesus has gone to Heaven to prepare a place for us that where He is, we may be also.**

> Peace I leave with you, my peace I give unto you: **not as the world giveth**, give I unto you. Let not your heart be troubled, neither let it be afraid.[32]

> Think not that I am come to send peace on earth: I came not to send peace, but a sword.[33]

> **For when they shall say, Peace and safety; then sudden destruction cometh upon them,** as travail upon a woman with child; and they shall not escape.[34]

> They are of the world: therefore speak they of the world, and the world heareth them. We are of God: he that knoweth God heareth us; he that is not of God heareth not us. Hereby know we the spirit of truth, and the spirit of error.[35]

---

31 Hebrews 9:22

32 John 14:27

33 Matthew 10:34; see also Luke 12:51

34 1 Thessalonians 5:3

35 1 John 4:5–6

(For an in-depth study of how this applies to Rick Warren's teachings, see Bob DeWaay's *Redefining Christianity: Understanding the Purpose-Driven Movement*.)

The world hates true Christians because their message is that God's peace plan requires repentance and reconciliation to Christ alone:

> If the world hate you, ye know that it hated me before it hated you.[36]

> Marvel not, my brethren, if the world hate you.[37]

> **Woe unto you, when all men shall speak well of you!** for so did their fathers to the false prophets.[38]

Wrath of the Lamb

Rick Warren's global PEACE plan is a dominionist,[39] "Kingdom Now" peace plan. He completely turns eschatology upside down, and what isn't upended has glaring omissions of critical biblical end-time passages! Only until the Captain of the Hosts, the true leader of the billion-man (or more) army, the Lord Himself descends, will the real global peace plan (the millennial kingdom) be inaugurated.[40]

Rick Warren's global PEACE plan contains no plan for de-

---

36 John 15:18

37 1 John 3:13

38 Luke 6:26

39 For an excellent article by Sarah Leslie on the relationship between Rick Warren's global PEACE plan to dominionism see: "Dominionism and the Rise of Christian Imperialism" — www.discernment-ministries.org/ChristianImperialism.htm

40 See Revelation 19-21; see also Dr. Noah Hutchings' *The Dark Side of the Purpose Driven Church*, p. 8.

stroying the Antichrist and False Prophet, and for binding Satan. Jesus Christ will destroy Antichrist and the False Prophet with the breath of His nostrils at — *and not before* — His return, and He will cast Satan into the bottomless pit for the thousand-year reign of His millennium.

If Warren's plan succeeds, it will leave most of the population on the earth intact, absent the wrath of the Lamb. Just prior to and in conjunction with the Lord's return, "There will be wars and at least one-half the world's population will be killed. . . ."[41]

Rick Warren consummates his final PEACE plan for the earth without war. But this is impossible, because the global peace that the Lord will personally bring to the earth when He returns will not happen until the Lord first sends the four horses of the apocalypse, in particular the red horse who will take peace from the earth: "And there went out another horse that was red: and power was given to him that sat thereon **to take peace from the earth**, and that they should kill one another: and there was given unto him a great sword."[42]

When the Lord returns, He will first make global war before He inaugurates his global peace plan, better known as the millennial thousand-year reign of Christ.

> And the kings of the earth, and the great men, and the rich men, and the chief captains, and the mighty men, and every bondman, and every free man, hid themselves in the dens and in the rocks of the mountains; And said to the mountains and rocks, Fall on us, and hide us from the face of him that sitteth on the throne, and from **the wrath of the Lamb**: For the great day of his wrath is come; and who shall be able to stand?[43]

---

41   Bible Believer's Evangelistic Association, "God's Plan for the Ages."

42   Revelation 6:4

43   Revelation 6:15–17

Even if the saints as the church could take dominion of the earth before the Lord's return, they could not do so until after the Antichrist is temporarily given power to make war against them and conquer them!! **"And it was given unto him to make war with the saints, and to overcome them**: and power was given him over all kindreds, and tongues, and nations."[44]

So there will be no permanent final global peace until these things be fulfilled. Then and only then will the scripture be fulfilled: "And the seventh angel sounded; and there were great voices in heaven, saying, **The kingdoms of this world are become the kingdoms of our Lord**, and of his Christ; and he shall reign for ever and ever."[45]

Curses

I have already addressed some of the glaring omissions in Rick Warren's global PEACE plan, but there are two contingencies for which he fails to account that would also prevent his plan from succeeding.

First, he does not mention that the reason the five "giants" he identifies exist in the first place is because of the curse in the Garden of Eden due to the fall of Adam. The whole earth is under judgment and will remain so until Christ returns to reverse the curse. It is not a question of what we can do to reverse the curse in an attempt to usher in global peace, but of *who* must reverse it. It can't happen until Christ returns to set up His kingdom. Warren's global PEACE plan is just another human potential movement.

Second, Warren does not mention the curse at the Tower of Babel where God confounded the languages. Prior to that time, the world spoke one language; an impostor peace plan is one which still retains the confusion of languages. This remains yet

---

44 Revelation 13:7

45 Revelation 11:15; see Revelation 19–20 for more details

another still-binding judgment of God on mankind. Rick Warren touts human potential, but human potential was at the core of why God destroyed the Tower of Babel. Had God not destroyed the tower, if the people desired, they could have achieved anything, including a global man-made peace plan.

The real global peace plan will be Christ's kingdom He sets up on earth when He returns. And when He does, He will reverse this curse as well. The Antichrist may attempt to do this, but anyone other than Christ Himself who tries doing it is a pretender.

Even if Rick Warren were to succeed in slaying his five giants (which he has guaranteed), his PEACE plan is still inferior to the peace plan the Lord Himself will set up. However, it lines up perfectly with Satan's peace plan. The counterfeit peace plan must first come, ushered in by the Antichrist, before the Lord's global peace will be ushered in by the Lord Himself. Christians should not buy into any global peace plan that will precede the Lord's worldwide peace plan.

We are instructed in the Lord's Prayer to pray, "thy kingdom come." Rick Warren promises us kingdom *now*! Jesus Christ told us that the time when He will set up His kingdom on earth is determined by the Father. Jesus Christ's global kingdom of peace cannot be set up until He restores the kingdom of Israel when He returns. Jerusalem will be the capital of the world, and Israel will be the preeminent nation on earth. It will not be determined by Rick Warren.

> When they therefore were come together, they asked of him, saying, Lord, wilt thou at this time restore again the kingdom to Israel? And he said unto them, **It is not for you to know the times or the seasons, which the Father hath put in his own power.**[46]

---

46   Acts 1:6–7

Chapter 3

What Is the Definition of Evil?

If anyone on the earth should be able to define "evil," it should be "America's pastor" . . . but this is not the case. Here are some excerpts of what Rick Warren said at a conference in July 2005 at the **Aspen Institute**, an organization that promotes the New Age [more accurately, the new world order], where he was a featured speaker on the panel entitled: "The Problem of Evil."[47]

> In fact, I don't think evil and sin are the same. . . . We don't know the answers . . . we really don't. . . . None of us are going to come out at the end of the day and say, "Got that one figured out." If you do, please write the book on it and I will buy it. . . . I don't think it [evil] is the same thing as sin. . . . I don't consider myself an evil person because I sin. . . . I think you have to reserve the word "evil" for "evil." . . . I haven't yet found a good definition of it. . . . Maybe Peter has. I was the one who suggested this topic, by the way, because I wanted to hear what Alan and Peter had to say about it because these are two men I have respected for years—read all their stuff—and I really came to take notes. . . . We can become an evil person by making bad choices. . . . I think evil is metastazation where it just takes over. . . .

47 July 8 morning session: *American Experience: The Problem of Evil*, with Rev. Peter Gomes and Pastor Rick Warren; moderator: Alan Wolfe. Aspen Institute Conference, July 8, 2005, compact disc.

Later on in this panel discussion, Rick Warren continued:

You're a good man [referring to Alan Wolfe] . . . **when we begin to compartmentalize our lives we're headed for evil [emphasis mine]**. . . . I don't act one way with Alan and another way over here with Mrs. Resnick and another way over here with Alan Simpson . . . okay? . . . I am the same no matter where I am. What you see is what you get. Rick Warren has integrity because he doesn't act one way with one crowd and another way with another crowd. He is integrated . . . and when what I see in our society today is a misunderstanding of character that thinks I can compartmentalize this area of my life and then go do this the next day and that's how they would justify it. And I think that total compartmentalization is a myth and moves us towards more and more evil. . . . As I pointed out yesterday, Abraham Lincoln and Washington said things that President Bush could never get away with today. There was far more God talk. Go to the second inaugural address of Lincoln. Read it in the Lincoln Memorial. And it is full of God is on our side talk.

I can't imagine any Christian wanting the pastor of their own church (let alone following him globally as the leader of hundreds of thousands of churches) to be someone who is still looking for a good definition of "evil." Scripture tells us that God's "people are destroyed for lack of knowledge."[48] We already have the ultimate authoritative book which defines "evil"and good: the Bible.

Rick Warren proceeds to remark that he doesn't know objectively what evil is, but that he would recognize it if he saw it. Are we to depend on his subjective assessment of what constitutes evil? We don't need Rick Warren's subjective assessment

---

48   Hosea 4:6

of what constitutes evil because we have the objective criteria. The word "evil" occurs 613 times in the King James Bible, and Scripture goes into elaborate detail defining and describing not only what evil is, but *who* is evil. Subjective definitions of evil produced gnosticism and mysticism, Christianity's earliest heresies, as evidenced by the teachings of the "desert fathers," now being imported into the church by Rick Warren and the emerging church movements.[49]

Contradicting his earlier statement that he could not find a good definition of evil, Rick Warren then goes on to define it by telling us that sin doesn't become evil until it metastasizes, that sin in and of itself is not yet evil. This may sound right, but is it? My father was a physician and often talked to me about the word metastasize, particularly as it corresponded to whether cancer was malignant. So when I heard Rick Warren describe the process and meaning of "metastasize," I knew he was wrong. Medically, *metastasize* is defined: "To spread to another part of the body, usually through the blood vessels, lymph channels or spinal fluid."[50]

This definition virtually echoes the scriptural process of unholy leaven in a lump, i.e., it spreads until the entire loaf is leavened. When Jesus warns us of the leaven of the Pharisees and Herod, and when the apostle Paul cautions that a little leaven leavens the whole lump, they are not saying that leaven is not evil or wicked until it spreads (i.e., while it is still small), but it is already evil at the beginning *before* it spreads throughout the entire lump. "Your glorying is not good. Know ye not that a little

---

49 For more information on "desert fathers," see: www.abrahamic-faith.com/James/ Part%20X%20Enneagram%20Profiling%20vs.%20Scripture%20Documentary.html and, "The Emergent Church," Albert James Dager, *Media Spotlight*, Volume 28, Number 4, 2005.

50 www.cancerweb.ncl.ac.uk/cgi-bin/ombd?metastasize

leaven leaveneth the whole lump?"[51]

From Rick Warren's analogy, we would be led to believe that sin is not evil until it spreads. But sin is evil, period! It does not need to spread (metastasize) to become evil. Even if this were true, who decides at which point of sins' spread now qualifies as evil? Rick Warren? Scripture?

It is supremely ironic that Rick Warren would give us this definition of evil, because later in the panel discussion Rick Warren warns of the danger of absolute power. He describes why there are three branches of government: to balance power and keep each branch in check. Yet he retains absolute sovereignty in his own church and trains thousands of purpose-driven churches to vest a single pastor with the authority to cast the vision for the church through Dan Sutherland's Church Transitions organization, which has already trained 100,000 church leaders. Warren should heed his own advice given on "Larry King Live": "You give a guy a little bit of power and they turn into Stalin."[52] And yet Rick Warren is quite forthright in announcing that he is going to be *the* general of his billion-man Christian army.[53]

Warren tells us Abraham Lincoln said that God is on our side, but that is not what Lincoln actually said. Here is Lincoln's comment from a conversation in the White House during the Civil War. Note that, in fact, Lincoln says quite the opposite of what Warren alleges: "Sir, my concern is not whether God is on our side; my greatest concern is to be on God's side, for God is always right."

Warren also referred to Lincoln's second inaugural address, where we can read just how much God was on our side.[54] (I did

---

51   1 Corinthians 5:6; see also Galatians 5:9

52   CNN, "Larry King Live," December 2, 2005

53   www.christianitytoday.com/ct/2005/0101/17.32.html

54   It can be found at www.bartleby.com/124/pres32.html

as Rick Warren suggested at the Aspen Conference—I looked up and read Lincoln's second inaugural address.) Nothing like what Warren states is in this address. Lincoln did quote Jesus Christ from Matthew 18:7: "The Almighty has His own purposes. 'Woe unto the world because of offenses; for it must needs be that offenses come, but woe to that man by whom the offense cometh.'"

A Christian leader or pastor should be able to discern evil and be a discerner of spirits. Otherwise, how does he detect doctrines of demons, false teachings, or when a wolf is in the sheepfold? If we are good Bereans, we can ferret out a false teacher using the objective criteria of Scripture. Rick Warren, by his own testimony, can't do that, so would we want him as "America's pastor" as *Time* has dubbed him? I don't think so!

Further, it is clear Rick Warren does not recognize a false teacher, or evil in his own midst (or at least does not mark him as such). Rev. Peter Gomes, his co-panelist, is openly gay,[55] and is a universalist (confirmed by him at the Aspen Conference when Rev. Gomes was asked about his new book). He is a professor and chairman of Christian morals at Harvard University, and a fellow of the Jesus Seminar (which thinks it can determine what parts of Scripture are authentic)—what a mockery of God! But Warren proclaims that he is a great admirer of Gomes and has read all his works.

Rick Warren's effusive praise of Peter Gomes is quite ironic, given that Warren now distances himself from Dr. Robert Schuller, who is also a universalist.[56] It is difficult to believe that Warren would discover that Schuller is a false teacher in only the last few years, when his full-blown heresies were in full public

---

55 www.creationists.org/resp0013.html

56 For proof of Dr. Robert Schuller's promotion of universalism, listen to the Southwest Radio Ministries interview of Warren Smith, December 15–16, 2005—www.swrc.com/broadcasts/2005/december.htm.

view in 1990 as he took his "self-esteem" gospel to Russia (a message mirrored in Warren's March 2005 *Ladies Home Journal* article). Schuller's departure from orthodox Christianity can be documented as early as 1982, when he published his well-known book entitled *Self-Esteem: The New Reformation*. (See the section in this document on "New Reformation.")

Rick Warren further states at the Aspen Conference that he does not compartmentalize, that he is the same before all audiences, and that he is not duplicitous. This statement is the height of absurdity! According to Warren's definition of evil, one who increasingly compartmentalizes his life would then render Warren evil by his own definition, as we read the doctrinal position statements of his Saddleback Church and then compare it to his March 2005 *Ladies Home Journal* column. You will clearly see how double-minded Rick Warren is.[57]

Who's Laughing?

Upon being informed of Neal Donald Walsch's New Age peace plan, during an interview *Rick Warren laughs*, then laughs again louder.[58]

Warren, who has been dubbed "America's pastor," and who is continually voted one or two in polls as to who is the most influential evangelical leader in America, should *grieve* at the many who will be led away from God by Neal Donald Walsch. Woe unto you who laugh now; blessed are those who mourn at the state of the world. Christian leaders (and all Christians) should follow the example of Jeremiah. He did not think what the leaders of Israel were doing to his people was very funny. There is not one single example of Jesus or any of His apostles laughing

---

57 www.newswithviews.com/PaulProctor/proctor66.htm

58 Richard Abanes, *Rick Warren and the Purpose That Drives Him*, (Harvest House 2005), p. 23

in the face of false teachings. Instead, they gave the strongest of warnings. Did the apostle Paul laugh when false teachers were threatening the church of Ephesus?

> Take heed therefore unto yourselves, and to all the flock, over the which the Holy Ghost hath made you overseers, to feed the church of God, which he hath purchased with his own blood. For I know this, that after my departing shall grievous wolves enter in among you, not sparing the flock. Also of your own selves shall men arise, speaking perverse things, to draw away disciples after them. **Therefore watch, and remember, that by the space of three years I ceased not to warn every one night and day with tears.**[59]

James 1:8 says that a "double-minded man is unstable in all his ways." Rick Warren does not and apparently *can* not discern good from evil, which may explain why he promotes false teacher after false teacher, as outlined in this document and the referenced resources. His own SHAPE program, based on the teachings of occultist Carl Jung who believed good and evil should be balanced and reconciled, belies the claim that Warren knows what he is talking about regarding the definition of evil, let alone the idea that he can be trusted to run a Christian global PEACE plan. When he does not blur the line between good and evil, he obliterates it. **"Woe unto them that call evil good, and good evil; that put darkness for light, and light for darkness; that put bitter for sweet, and sweet for bitter!"** [60]

If the Lord Himself through Isaiah gives such a dire warning about calling evil good and good evil, wouldn't it be wise for all

59   Acts 20:28-31; see also "Another Possible Gospel of Robert Schuller's" — www.letusreason.org/Poptea1.htm

60   Isaiah 5:20

Christians to heed this warning? And how are we to heed it if we "don't really have any good definition of evil"? Most assuredly, we don't want a pastor who doesn't have a handle on the definition himself. We certainly don't want to anoint him "America's pastor." A host of Christians do not abide with this title.

For an excellent chart on Rick Warren's leaven, see Greg DeVoignes "Hidden Leaven in the Church Growth Movement: How it got in" by Christian Research Ministries.[61] For a list of churches in your state or country which have *already* imported the purpose-driven leaven, go to the Simplicity In Christ website.[62]

---

61 www.crmspokane.org/cgm_chart.htm

62 www.purposedriven.com/en-US/40DayCampaigns/PDCampaignChurchFinder. htm—This list is not exhaustive, as there are many churches who have run 40 Days of Purpose or other Warren programs which are not listed in this search engine.

Chapter 4

Who's Leading?

Rick Warren expects to train and lead a billion-man Christian army.[63] The obvious fuzzy math problem with this proclamation is that there aren't that many true Christians on the earth — the majority will choose the wide highway to Hell:

> Because strait is the gate, and narrow is the way, which leadeth
> unto life, and few there be that find it.[64]

> I tell you that he will avenge them speedily. Nevertheless when
> the Son of man cometh, shall he find faith on the earth?[65]

Warren's global PEACE plan contains no enforcement clause or declaration of who will enforce it, whereas in Jesus Christ's worldwide peace plan, Jesus Himself will rule with a rod of iron: "And she brought forth a man child, who was to rule all nations with a rod of iron: and her child was caught up unto God, and to his throne."[66]

It is Jesus Christ who will enforce the rule of *all* the nations, including the global governing of his worldwide plan of peace

---

63   www.wayoflife.org/fbns/rickwarren-globalvision.html

64   Matthew 7:14; see also Matthew 20:16; 22:14

65   Luke 18:8

66   Revelation 12:5

(i.e., the millennium). He will not be initiating Rick Warren's global PEACE plan; He will be enforcing His own.

New Reformation

Rick Warren says his global PEACE plan is the New Reformation.[67] However, Robert Schuller already said his self-esteem gospel is the New Reformation. He even wrote a book about it nearly twenty-five years before Rick Warren's plan.[68]

What does Rick Warren mean? As Christian author Warren Smith points out: "The problems weren't new, but . . . his PEACE plan methodology of confronting these 'Giants' would be a revolution."[69]

In Rick Warren's plan, PEACE is an acronym for Planting Church, Equipping Leaders, Assisting the Poor, Caring for the Sick, and Educating the Next Generation. The five "giants" he refers to which he plans to obliterate are: spiritual emptiness, egocentric leadership, extreme poverty, pandemic diseases, and illiteracy and education.

> Even in villages where you cannot find a clinic, a store, a school, or a post office, you can often find a church. The PEACE plan will address these five "giant" problems by Planting new churches . . . Equipping leaders . . . Assisting the poor . . . Caring for the sick . . . and Educating the next generation. . . . I now believe that I know why God is blessing this book [*The Purpose Driven Life*] in such an unusual way. It is more than just a message that God wants to get out to everyone (which is huge). I now also see that God is using this phenomena to expand the

---

67   www.abpnews.com/485.article.print

68   Robert Schuller, *Self-Esteem: The New Reformation* (Word Books, Waco, 1982)

69   Warren Smith, *Deceived on Purpose,* p. 126

platform for us to mobilize thousands of local churches for
global world missions through the PEACE plan.[70]

From a Christian biblical perspective, global evangelism has
always been the mission of the true church. However, this must
be qualified. The church is led by elders who then equip the
saints. In addition, the biblical references to the poor and sick
refer first and foremost to saints of the household of God, and
then to our enemies.

In promoting his plan, Warren is redefining the mission of the
church. His idea is that we are to wipe out world problems and
make the world a better place to live before Christ returns. His
program screams of dominionist theology[71] which teaches that
Christ can't return until the church takes over the earth. And his
billion-man army reminds me of two other "army" movements
in the name of Jesus: the Army of Joel and the Manifest Sons of
God, both of which promote false teaching; they think the Lord
has given them a mandate to take over the earth for Jesus so that
He can return.

Though "P" for Church Planting can still be found on Rick
Warren's website describing his global PEACE plan, he changed
the acronym to have "P" stand for "Participation" in his keynote
speech at the Religious Newswriters convention on September
29, 2005,[72] where Warren states that he is getting 400,000 churches
to participate in his plan. The mission of the church as defined
in Matthew 28, Luke 24, and Acts 1 is to preach the gospel and
call people out of the world. Once converted, people are taught

---

70   www.saddleback.com/home/todaystory.asp?id=6213 (removed)

71   For a good expose on dominionist and reconstructionist theology, see Bob DeWaay's
     CIC article entitled "The Dominion Mandate and the Christian Reconstruction
     Movement" — www.cicministry.org/scholarly/sch001.htm

72   www.rna.org/meetingdates.php#miamithursday

to "obey everything that Jesus taught." Part of this teaching is giving alms, but that is hardly the key mission of the church, as Warren claims. In fact, Christ tells us *not* to give alms before men to be seen by men; Warren brags about his almsgiving to the whole world.

From a worldly perspective, history is replete with peace plans and men of peace—even those claiming the name of Jesus. Rick Warren thinks Muslims can help his peace plan with "spiritual lostness" (see chapter 7) in spite of the fact that they themselves are totally lost. Warren's plan is not new; it is simply revisionist history. It is titled: "God's Dream for You—and the World."[73]

God never sleeps, so God doesn't dream (who could give God a dream?)! But even were God to have given Rick Warren his dream, God gives instructions which are 100 percent truth, not any percent falsehood! One should also note that the dreams God does give—even to non-believers in God—primarily are warnings and deal with judgment.

Guaranteed Success

Rick Warren says:

The Global PEACE Plan **is going to happen.**[74]

You are not a part of Saddleback Church by accident. . . . I say this without fear of exaggeration—God is going to use you, and all of us together at Saddleback, to change history![75]

God says of boasting about tomorrow:

---

73   Warren Smith, *Deceived on Purpose*, p. 123.

74   Ibid, p. 124

75   Ibid, p. 129

Boast not thyself of to morrow; for thou knowest not what a day may bring forth.[76]

Go to now, ye that say, To day or to morrow we will go into such a city, and continue there a year, and buy and sell, and get gain: Whereas ye know not what shall be on the morrow. For what is your life? It is even a vapour, that appeareth for a little time, and then vanisheth away. For that ye ought to say, If the Lord will, we shall live, and do this, or that. But now ye rejoice in your boastings: all such rejoicing is evil. Therefore to him that knoweth to do good, and doeth it not, to him it is sin.[77]

Other scriptural warnings against presumption include: Genesis 11:4; Numbers 14:44; 15:30; 20:11; Deuteronomy 6:16; 18:20; 2 Chronicles 26:16; Isaiah 45:9; Luke 12:19; 1 Corinthians 10:9; and 2 Peter 2:10.

---

76 Proverbs 27:1

77 James 4:13–17

Chapter 5

How Is It Financed?

Rick Warren's global PEACE plan's initial funding is generated by the royalties he receives from his book, *The Purpose Driven Life*, and tithes and offerings from Saddleback Church in California. He also promotes reverse tithing.[78] Additional income is derived from his companion books and study guides, as well as the 115,000 pastors who subscribe to his pastors.com "Rick Warren Ministry Toolbox" and pay to download his sermons. However, this is just seed money; his global PEACE plan will require funding vastly exceeding what has currently been financed if it is to transform every nation on earth. To fully succeed, Rick Warren is going to have to forge alliances with heads of state, corporations, and nongovernmental organizations (NGOs).

I am utterly astonished that someone could write a book saturated with false teachings, promotion of false teachers, false translations, and even blueprints for how to practice psychology, and then validate his own righteousness by declaring repeatedly how he is going to give 90 percent of the royalty income from his sales back to the church, charities, and of course, to finance his global PEACE plan. Rick Warren has made his fortune by "causing my little children to stumble," deceiving 30 million readers of his *Purpose Driven Life* book, leading astray 20,000 members of his own church, 400,000 church leaders he has trained, 20,000

---

78   www.beliefnet.com/story/177/story_17718

churches in a host of denominations, and 165 countries, which he hopes to turn into purpose-driven countries under the banner of his global PEACE plan.[79]

We also constantly hear of how modestly Rick Warren lives. This reminds me of the Vatican. The pope isn't rich; the wealth is held by the Roman Catholic Church. However, as the absolute sovereign authority over its assets and distribution of funds, does he need to technically own anything? Likewise, Rick Warren has absolute authority over Saddleback Church and his global PEACE plan. He is simply taking money from one pocket and putting it in the other; it is still in the same pair of pants. It would not matter if Rick Warren gained the whole world from the sales of his book and gave all of it to finance his global PEACE plan, if his fortune was made from a book of false teachings. Warren should refund the money from his books sales, and his publisher, Zondervan, needs to remand and recall his book! Further, Christians and churches who bought his book should strongly consider having a bonfire and pitching his books into it, as the early Christians did in Acts 19:19 when they burned all of their magic arts scrolls.

Rick Warren has rejected correction and refused to make restitution—the fruit of repentance. Even if there were such a person as "America's pastor," Rick Warren has not met the first essential criteria: being faithful to God's Word. As a pastor, he must meet the requirement of an elder, to be able to rightly divide the truth.[80] A true elder must defend, contend, and confess the faith without equivocation or waffling. It is bad enough that much of Warren's income was received from unsuspecting nonbelievers who could not discern the falsehood of his teachings.

79 www.bpnews.net/bpnews.asp?ID=20603

80 For the qualifications of an elder, see 1 Timothy 3:2–7; Titus 1:6–7; and "The Pastor Is Master, Isn't He?"

Even worse, he has plundered from tens of thousands of church treasuries and individual Christians who bought his book. Some prominent Christian leaders who should know better say that before Jesus ever criticized anyone, He always found something good to say about them. This is inaccurate. Jesus did this with individual churches, as with five of the seven churches in Revelation, but He never did this with a false teacher. Neither did any of the prophets of the Old Testament, nor any of the apostles in the New Testament. *Never!* Christian leaders who defend Rick Warren think that giving profits to charity somehow sanctifies Warren's false teachings in the book which generated the royalties. Furthermore, even if the income came from honest gain, tithing should be voluntary. Warren forces members of his own church to sign tithing covenants,[81] putting Christians back under the law. The apostle Paul condemned the Galatian church for doing that.

Paul teaches that we are *not* to give out of compulsion, but this doesn't stop Rick Warren. It would be bad enough were he to require this only of his own megachurch, but he trains leaders in his purpose-driven church franchises to do the same. This still doesn't take into account the destruction left in Warren's wake in all of the churches who paid for his *Purpose Driven Life* book and materials, to facilitate transition from a New Testament church model to purpose-driven church polity. Many members of these churches did not just lose twenty dollars paying for one of Warren's books; they lost their church or were purpose-driven out. In many cases, these were senior members or charter members who had helped build their church. I wonder what all those saints forced out of their churches thought when Rick Warren had the audacity to state the following on "Larry King Live" on CNN: "One is a reformation of the church in America and the other is

---

81   www.letusreason.org/BookR12.htm

a return of civility to society when people who disagree can still get along and like each other even if they disagree."[82]

For documented case studies of the consequences for Christians who opposed Rick Warren's teachings and refusal to sign his covenants, see the article entitled "Spiritual Euthanasia."[83] Also see Bob DeWaay's *Redefining Christianity: Understanding the Purpose-Driven Movement,* and Dr. Noah Hutchings' *The Dark Side of the Purpose Driven Church.*

Rick Warren tells us how much he is giving to the church and repeatedly advertises this in the market place. So, let's see what the Lord commands regarding this practice:

> **Take heed that ye do not your alms before men, to be seen of them: otherwise ye have no reward of your Father which is in heaven.** Therefore when thou doest thine alms, **do not sound a trumpet before thee**, as the hypocrites do in the synagogues and in the streets, that they may have glory of men. Verily I say unto you, They have their reward. But when thou doest alms, let not thy left hand know what thy right hand doeth: **That thine alms may be in secret: and thy Father which seeth in secret himself shall reward thee openly.**[84]

As bad as it is how Rick Warren made his fortune in the first place, as bad as it is that he touts it before men, as bad as it is what happened to a host of saints who resisted his teachings and takeover of churches, and as bad as it is that the unholy leaven of Warren's teachings has virtually if not permanently taken over once God-fearing sound doctrine churches, imagine the greater consequences for using the income from his false teachings and

---

82 CNN, "Larry King Live," December 2, 2005

83 www.letusreason.org/Current61.htm

84 Matthew 6:1-4

spiritual abuse of authority to finance the components of his global PEACE plan outlined in this document. Warren may succeed with his global PEACE plan; after all, he has guaranteed it. But what will be the cost? Who will pick up the pieces of the dismembered Christians left chewed up by the propeller in the wake of his global PEACE plan once it is consummated?

There is no room at Rick Warren's table for those Christians he calls "resisters." Dan Sutherland of Church Transitions, his co-conspirator, calls leaders who oppose or question this movement "Sanballats,"[85] referring to a prominent Samaritan who was a persistent and serious enemy to Nehemiah during the time of the Jews' rebuilding of Jerusalem after their return from the Babylonian exile. But there will be room at the table for all true saints who will take their place when they sit at the wedding supper of the Lamb.[86]

---

85 Bob DeWaay, *Redefining Christianity*, p. 57.

86 See Matthew 26:26–29 and Revelation 19:19.

Chapter 6

Israel

Warren has already approved his *Purpose Driven Life* book being translated into Hebrew by MAOZ Ministries (distributed in Israel).[87] The long term impact of MAOZ Ministry in Israel presenting Warren's *Purpose Driven Life* book into Hebrew is ominous:

Warren is already in the process of turning Rwanda into a Purpose Driven country with his global PEACE plan, and he now has his sights set on Israel. His idea of a global PEACE plan is to go into a village and form an alliance with a "man of peace." This could be a Muslim cleric in charge of the Temple Mount. Were Arafat (winner of the Nobel Peace Prize) still alive, he would have been "the man of peace" for the Palestinians. He would not sign the last peace plan because he said he would be assassinated for giving up absolute rule of the Temple Mount in Jerusalem, which he said belonged in total to all Muslims.

This book campaign by MAOZ will help pave the way for Warren to get Israel to sign one of his peace plan covenants to convert Israel into a purpose-driven country. (Remember, Rick Warren's plan is global, so it must include Israel).

Warren has already formed an unholy alliance with the United Nations and even brags how they are interested in his

---

87   October 29, 2005, e-mail from Cookie Schwaeber-Issan, Partner Relations Maoz Israel, maozisrael@maozisrael.org. — MAOZ website is www.maozisrael.org.

PEACE plan. Here is some recent proof that the United Nations is the enemy of Israel:

> The United Nations held a "Day of Solidarity with the Palestinian People" last week. A large map of "Palestine," with Israel literally wiped off the map, featured prominently in the festivities. The ceremony was held at the UN headquarters in New York and was attended by Secretary General Kofi Annan and the Presidents of the UN Security Council and the General Assembly. During the festivities, a map labeled a "map of Palestine" was displayed prominently between UN and PLO flags. The map, with "Palestine" written in Arabic atop it, does not include Israel, a member of the UN for 56 years.[88]

Let us take warning about the "man of peace" who will sign a covenant with Israel with this scriptural prophecy:

> And through his policy also he shall cause craft to prosper in his hand; and **he shall magnify himself in his heart, and by peace shall destroy many**: he shall also stand up against the Prince of princes; but he shall be broken without hand.[89]

> **And he shall confirm the *covenant* with many for one week:** and in the midst of the week he shall cause the sacrifice and the oblation to cease, and for the overspreading of abominations he shall make it desolate, even until the consummation, and that determined shall be poured upon the desolate.[90]

---

88 Arutz Sheva, December 8, 2005 — www.israelnn.com/news.php3?id=94461 Special thanks to December 10, 2005, Be Alert Newsletter.

89 Daniel 8:25

90 Daniel 9:27

Also see Psalm 83,[91] which describes what the Lord is going to do to the surrounding nations who will come to take plunder of Israel.

Rick Warren's global PEACE plan is a plan put in place without addressing Jacob's trouble (see Jeremiah 30:7), which must *first* come before the Lord's global kingdom of the Prince of Peace is established on earth!

Take warning! We must be on guard against *the* "man of peace" who will destroy many with peace—a man who loves covenants and enforces them. Will it be the covenant with Israel? This man of peace will do away with resisters to his peace plan and those who refuse to sign his covenant. Rick Warren has already trained tens of thousands of pastors how to get rid of what he calls "resisters" and "pillars" who would refuse to sign his covenants. We have already witnessed what happens to saints in a host of denominations who dare to oppose his teachings and refuse to sign his covenants.[92]

---

91   www.acwitness.org/psalm83english.html

92   www.abrahamic-faith.com/False-Teachers.html
     see also Dr. Noah Hutchings' *The Dark Side of the Purpose Driven Church*, p. 8

Chapter 7

Muslims

In an interview at The Pew Forum on Religion and Public Life, in describing his global PEACE plan, Rick Warren states in reference to "they" (referring to leaders in any village in the world that Rick Warren will recruit to participate in his global PEACE plan): "They don't have to be a Christian. In fact, **they could be a Muslim.**"[93]

Here is more regarding his position on Islam:

> **"I would trust any imam** or priest or rabbi to know what is going on in a community before I would any government agency."
> But, powerful as churches can be in working for the powerless, they can't succeed without governments and nongovernmental organizations, Warren said. Warren predicts that fundamentalism, of all varieties, will be "one of the big enemies of the 21st century. . . . Muslim fundamentalism, Christian fundamentalism, Jewish fundamentalism, secular fundamentalism — they're all motivated by fear. Fear of each other."[94]

In a feeble attempt at damage control, Rick Warren's staff has issued a release in which he tries to distance himself from calling Christian fundamentalists enemies of the twenty-first century.

---

93   www.pewforum.org/events/index.php?EventID=80%20page%2016

94   Paul Nussbaum, *Philadelphia Inquirer,* January 8, 2006

But Paul Proctor easily demolishes this attempt in his article entitled "Rick Warren—Fundamentalist or Finagler?"[95]

Proctor's article further corroborates all of Warren's duplicity concerning his comments at the Aspen Institute. What is ironic is that Warren's new definition of fundamentalism is *exactly* what his programs are—more rules, myths, and traditions of men added to the burdens of Christians and enforced by his binding covenants!

One of the pillars of Warren's global PEACE plan is to "Plant Churches," even though, depending on his audience, he says the "P" stands for "participation." But it should be obvious to every Christian that **Muslims don't *plant* churches**. They wouldn't plant churches any more than they would build a Jewish temple or synagogue. Though there are Christian churches in some Arab countries, there are none in Saudi Arabia, the center of Islam. In fact, the Islamic "global peace plan" is to destroy churches. In Islamic law, according to the Koran and the Haddiths, there is no room for Jews, Christians, or a Jewish nation. Their global peace plan divides the world into two spheres: the House of Peace (submission) and the House of War. Once all infidels (yes, that's us) are destroyed, there will only be the House of Peace (submission). It won't contain the nation of Israel, and it won't have Jesus sitting on David's throne.

Matching the apostle John's own definition of the spirit of the antichrist, Islam does not believe that Jesus Christ is God who came in the flesh. Rick Warren is proposing unholy alliances with not just Islam, but any religion which qualifies as a candidate according to these scriptures:

> Who is a liar but he that denieth that Jesus is the Christ? He is **antichrist**, that denieth the Father and the Son.[96]

95   www.newswithviews.com/PaulProctor/proctor90.htm

96   1 John 2:22

And every spirit that confesseth not that Jesus Christ is come in the flesh is not of God: and this is that spirit of **antichrist**, whereof ye have heard that it should come; and even now already is it in the world.[97]

For many deceivers are entered into the world, who confess not that Jesus Christ is come in the flesh. This is a deceiver and an **antichrist**.[98]

Be ye not unequally yoked together with unbelievers: for what fellowship hath righteousness with unrighteousness? and what communion hath light with darkness? And what concord hath Christ with Belial? or what part hath he that believeth with an infidel? And what agreement hath the temple of God with idols? for ye are the temple of the living God; as God hath said, I will dwell in them, and walk in them; and I will be their God, and they shall be my people. Wherefore come out from among them, and be ye separate, saith the Lord, and touch not the unclean thing; and I will receive you.[99]

Rick Warren bases this component of his peace plan on this scripture: "And if the son of peace be there, your peace shall rest upon it: if not, it shall turn to you again."[100] However, this scripture actually refutes Warren's contention. Even if this "man of peace" were a Muslim, he would have to repent of being a Muslim and be born again as a believer in the Creator/Messiah Jesus Christ and renounce Islam. "Thou wilt keep him in perfect peace, whose

---

97   1 John 4:3

98   2 John 7

99   2 Corinthians 6:14–17

100   Luke 10:6

mind is stayed on thee: because he trusteth in thee.[101]" A Muslim's mind certainly is not stayed on Jesus Christ, our only Lord and Saviour, but on Allah! Yet Rick Warren believes a Muslim in any village could help him build his global PEACE plan.

For more information and scriptural support describing Islam's plan for global peace and worldwide domination, see "Muslim Jesus vs. Biblical Jesus."[102] Here is a list of twenty comparisons addressed in this article between the Islamic Jesus whom Muslims call "Isa" and the biblical Jesus. The Islamic position on the identity of Jesus is taken from the Koran and Haddiths, which together comprise the ultimate authority in Islam. Most Muslims are not aware of most of these texts. Likewise, most Christians are not thoroughly versed in their own biblical scriptures defending or describing the identity of Christ, let alone the Islamic scriptures describing Christ.

Muslim Jesus vs. Biblical Jesus:
Twenty Scriptural Reasons Why They Are Not the Same Jesus
A Compilation and Comparison by James Sundquist

1. Islamic Jesus was created and not eternal
2. Islamic Jesus is not the Lamb of God who was slain
3. Islamic Jesus will not return until Judgment Day
4. Islamic Jesus prophesied (but did not send) the coming of Mohammed (Islamic Jesus did not send the Holy Spirit)
5. Islam says salvation is found only in the five pillars of Islam
6. Islamic Jesus is an involuntary slave to Allah
7. Islamic Jesus was never crucified and therefore was not resurrected

---

101   Isaiah 26:3

102   www.erwm.com/muslim_jesus_vs_biblical_jesus.htm

8. Islamic Jesus is not God in the flesh as the Messiah
9. Islamic Jesus cannot be worshiped
10. Islamic Jesus not fit to be intercessor
11. Islamic Jesus will judge by the law of the Koran and not by the gospel
12. Islamic Jesus is simply another prophet
13. Islamic Jesus lands on a minaret in Damascus, Syria
14. Islamic Jesus returns on the wings of two angels
15. Islamic Jesus destroys Antichrist at Lydda (in Israel)
16. Islamic Jesus who returns will not be pierced
17. Islamic Jesus will marry a woman and have children
18. Islamic Jesus will break every cross
19. Islamic Jesus will die forty years after his return
20. Re: LOVE — there is no concept of agape love found in either the Koran or the Haddiths

See the full article for the scriptural truth compared to the lies from the writings of Islam.[103] I strongly encourage you to read Simon Altaf's new book entitled *Yeshua or Isa?* Simon Altaf is a former Sunni Muslim, now a devout Christian and scholar. He concurs that it is impossible for any Muslim to be a candidate for Rick Warren's global PEACE plan.[104]

Islam also has a completely different angel Gabriel than the Bible teaches. Islam teaches that Gabriel said that Mohammed is the Comforter referred to in our Scripture. The Bible teaches that Gabriel announces the birth of Jesus our Messiah. But it was Jesus who then said that the Holy Spirit is the Comforter that Jesus alone would send. This was confirmed and fulfilled in the book of Acts at Pentecost, several hundred years before Mohammed was even born.

---

103   Courtesy *Be Alert* newsletter, Moriel Ministries, November 5, 2005 — www.berean-beacon.org/articles/muslim_vs_biblical_jesus.htm

104   *Yeshua or Isa?* is now available at www.abrahamic-faith.com/Books/y.html

And I will pray the Father, and he shall give you another **Comforter**, that he may abide with you for ever.[105]

But **the Comforter**, which is the Holy Ghost, whom the Father will send in my name, he shall teach you all things, and bring all things to your remembrance, whatsoever I have said unto you.[106]

But when **the Comforter** is come, whom I will send unto you from the Father, even the Spirit of truth, which proceedeth from the Father, he shall testify of me.[107]

Nevertheless I tell you the truth; It is expedient for you that I go away: for if I go not away, **the Comforter** will not come unto you; but if I depart, I will send him unto you.[108]

But ye shall receive power, after that the **Holy Ghost** is come upon you: and ye shall be witnesses unto me both in Jerusalem, and in all Judaea, and in Samaria, and unto the uttermost part of the earth.[109]

Muslims have beheaded Christians and Jews for fifteen hundred years and will be responsible for the beheading of Christians in the Antichrist's global empire, believing they are doing God a favor:

And I saw thrones, and they sat upon them, and judgment was given unto them: and I saw the souls of them that were

---

105 John 14:16

106 John 14:26

107 John 15:26

108 John 16:7

109 Acts 1:8

beheaded for the witness of Jesus, and for the word of God, and which had not worshipped the beast, neither his image, neither had received his mark upon their foreheads, or in their hands; and they lived and reigned with Christ a thousand years.[110]

Finally, if Islam has the same Jesus and Islam is a religion of peace, then why was an Afghanistani man recently on trial, under Sharia Islamic law, for converting from Islam to Christianity? If convicted, the sentence is death. The case was dismissed for lack of evidence, but the law is still part of the country's constitution.

The fact remains, Islam has a different Jesus, a different Gabriel, a different comforter, and a different peace plan. Yet Rick Warren is willing to form alliances with Muslims to implement his global PEACE plan.

---

110   Revelation 20:4

Chapter 8

Abuse of Authority

Nehemiah's Covenant

Rick Warren uses the fact that Nehemiah invoked a covenant in Israel in the Old Testament as a rationale that he has the right to invoke them in the church. In the following interview, Richard Abanes asks Warren: "Why do you have covenants? Some people say they're cultic."

Rick Warren replies: "Is the Nicene Creed cultic?"[111] He then says, "This weekend, I'll unveil our global PEACE plan."[112]

So was this PEACE plan of Rick Warren's like the Council of Nicea for the whole world, where many Christian leaders met to represent all Christians? Surely a key difference is that the Nicene Creed isn't a covenant. It is a statement of faith, a summary of beliefs and doctrines outlined in Scripture, reflecting orthodox Christianity, not a promise about certain church ordinances. This can't be compared to Rick Warren's covenants. Warren has made a false analogy. Ironically, the Nicene Creed was the product of an ultimatum set down by Emperor Constantine (another example of the leaven of Herod) in A.D. 325. In like manner, Rick Warren forces compliance with his own covenants.

Nehemiah's covenant was a renewal of an existing covenant, not a new one. In addition, the existing covenant was God's, not

---

111   Richard Abanes, *Rick Warren and the Purpose that Drives Him,* p. 31

112   Warren Smith, *Deceived on Purpose,* p. 124

man's. The laws enumerated in chapters nine and ten of Nehemiah were laws already given by God to the Israelites through Moses. Note in verse 29 of chapter ten that the covenant was also a curse, and the oath was to bind themselves back to the law of Moses and back to its curses.

Warren is seeking to put his congregation back under the law—the very thing Paul condemned the churches in Galatia for attempting to do! What was Rick Warren thinking? His list of requirements were *not* given by God to the church, but by Rick Warren himself. In fact, they defy Christ's own commands regarding oaths. Even Nehemiah did not take the draconian measures against the Israelites who did *not* sign the covenant that Rick Warren has trained purpose-driven church pastors and purpose-driven churches to do with members who refuse to sign his covenants.

Imagine what Nehemiah would think of Rick Warren holding negotiations with an Islamic leader in Jerusalem regarding the desirability of Nehemiah building a wall around Jerusalem. Israel should mark Rick Warren as a national security threat! In defending covenants, Rick Warren compares the relationship of a Christian and the church to a marriage. Such a comparison would lead us to believe that Christians are the bride of Christ and the church is the groom. This violates every passage in Scripture which clearly states that Christ is **the Groom.** The church is simply the collection of individual Christians who comprise the as-yet-unconsummated bride of Christ. This false analogy is one of the most important keys to see how Rick Warren has deceived the church into swearing loyalty to him and the pastors he recruits in churches throughout the world.

Warren's mandatory covenant creates misplaced loyalty and a false foundation for church government, completely corrupting the church and those who sign on to Warren's form of government. For more information exposing the fatal flaws of this type of church government and polity, see "Pastor Is Master, Isn't He?" You can also listen to Rick Warren's interview on the "Drew Marshall Show" and this author's response to Rick Warren (July 2).[113]

There is only one New Covenant for Christians! See Jesus Christ's and the apostle James' warnings about more oaths and covenants beyond the New Covenant![114]

Abuse of Authority

Documentation and case studies of the consequences of refusing to sign Rick Warren's covenants and opposing his teachings can be found in the following:

"Spiritual Euthanasia"
Media Spotlight
Vol. 28, No. 3, Summer 2005, Page 13
Al Dager — Director

Redefining Christianity:
Understanding the Purpose-Driven Movement
Bob DeWaay
21st Century Press, 2006

The Dark Side of the Purpose Driven Church
Noah W. Hutchings
Bible Belt Publishing, 2005[115]

In spite of the pandemic abuse of spiritual authority documented above, the Council for Christian Colleagues and Universities is

---

113   www.abrahamic-faith.com/False-Teachers.html

114   Matthew 5:33-37; James 5:12; see also chapter two of *Who's Driving the Purpose Driven Church?* (Bible Belt Publishing, 2005)

115   www.swrc.com

now adding insult to injury — a reproach to all of these victims —
by awarding Rick and Kay Warren the Mark O. Hatfield Award
for Christian Leadership at the 2006 CCCU International Forum
on Christian Higher Education.[116] The CCCU did go through with
giving this award to Rick Warren, in spite of the documentation
this author sent concerning him. There has been no response to
the subsequent follow-up I sent to them on Rick Warren.

False Teachings and False Bible Translations

Rick Warren's global PEACE plan is built on the foundation of his
Purpose Driven Church book, *Purpose Driven Life* book (sold over 30
million copies), and his Discovery 101, 201, 301 (SHAPE), and 401
classes. His global PEACE plan is the outgrowth of his Discovery
401 class, which is the global component, though everything he
teaches has already gone global. Discovery Class 401 is a more
detailed blueprint involving the nations of the world.

"God accepts me as I already am," according to Rick Warren's
March 2005 *Ladies Home Journal* column — and in his series every month after that first article. See Paul Proctor's article, "It's
Your Choice."[117] This is diametrically and diabolically opposed
to Scripture:

He that hath the Son hath life; and he that hath not the Son of
God hath not life.[118]

He that believeth on the Son hath everlasting life: and he that
believeth not the Son shall not see life; but the **wrath of God
abideth** on him.[119]

---

116 www.cccu.org/news/newsID.387/news_detail.asp

117 www.newswithviews.com/PaulProctor/proctor66.htm

118 1 John 5:12

119 John 3:36

For more information documenting Rick Warren's own false teachings, see chapter four of *Who's Driving the Purpose Driven Church?* See also sites documenting Rick Warren's false translations of the Bible,[120] chapter three of *Who's Driving the Purpose Driven Church?*, and "What Are the Roots of Purpose Driven Church" color chart.[121]

Secrecy

Rick Warren's global PEACE plan is built on the foundation of his purpose-driven church teachings, which include secretly introducing heresies into the church by training leaders (while not telling the congregation) how to remove "resisters" and "pillars" in the church and forcing members to sign his covenants. Here is an example from a long-time member of a church in Michigan:

> The pastor and the rest of the "staff" disappeared for a week to some secret Southern location and none could "disclose" the reason. "Top secret," without the congregation knowing anything about where they went or why they went, but it was to obtain training in Rick Warren's leadership principles on how deal with anyone opposing Rick Warren's teachings.
> Location:
> Safe Harbor Church
> 3552 South Pipestone Rd.
> Sodus , MI 49126 — a Church of God Prophecy Church

And here is what has been going on at Grace Assembly in Wake Forest, North Carolina:

> Resisters were pushed out not just for opposing Rick Warren,

120 www.despatch.cth.com/au/Articles_V/The_Message_E_Petersen.htm
www.newswithviews.com/BeritKjos/kjos22.htm

121 www.abrahamic-faith.com/James/charts.html

but for merely asking what was going on, or for pointing out error. It is now evident that some were removed because they actually resisted the "Transitioning" methods. Many left on their own, not really understanding the undercurrents, but after being hurt by being removed from their positions, sometimes learning about their removal from someone else, or even in the church bulletin! If covenants were required, it was only on staff. I have been told that staff members were not to talk about certain things. My estimate of departed members/attendees is between 45 and 60, most of them staffers or leadership and/or volunteer workers from a church of 150 to 200. There are many more who came and left quickly, before becoming involved.[122]

And here is what Scripture says about secret things: "The secret things belong unto the LORD our God: but those things which are revealed belong unto us and to our children for ever, that we may do all the words of this law."[123]

The secret things belong to God, not to Rick Warren, who privily (secretly) introduces these heresies in churches, just like Safe Harbor (which is no longer a safe harbor). The saints there couldn't defend themselves until it was too late!

And that because of false brethren unawares brought in, who came in **privily** to spy out our liberty which we have in Christ Jesus, that they might bring us into bondage.[124]

But there were false prophets also among the people, even as there shall be false teachers among you, who **privily** shall bring

---

122 Source: Leon O'Dell, e-mail address: kuvanant@earthlink.net

123 Deuteronomy 29:29

124 Galatians 2:4

in damnable heresies, even denying the Lord that bought them, and bring upon themselves swift destruction.[125]

Wherefore, if I come, I will remember his deeds which he doeth, prating against us with malicious words: and not content therewith, **neither doth he himself receive the brethren, and forbiddeth them that would, and casteth them out of the church.**[126]

I wrote unto the church: but Diotrephes, who loveth to have the preeminence among them, receiveth us not.[127]

Perfect Peace or Imperfect Peace?

Rick Warren said that as his plan was developed and perfected, it would be shared with all of the other churches around the world. Warren's five-step PEACE plan format is similar to one proposed by New Age leader Neale Donald Walsch, who also claimed to be inspired by God.[128]

Rick Warren's PEACE Plan and Other Teachings Copied from Others

- SHAPE was already created by Joe Weider (fitness giant)
- Purpose Driven already published by Tony Robbins (search Amazon for details)
- Personality Profile ("P") in SHAPE already conceived by Carl Jung
- 5–point PEACE plan already conceived by Neale Donald Walsh

---

125 2 Peter 2:1

126 3 John 10

127 3 John 19

128 Warren Smith, *Deceived on Purpose*, p. 127–128.

♦ God's Dream (Robert Schuller and Bruce Wilkinson)

God's peace plan and blueprint is original and perfect and already given by divine revelation of Scripture. By contrast, Rick Warren first gets input from non-Christians and pagan leaders to formulate his peace plan, *then* he tells the churches.[129] He will share it with them after seeking counsel from the ungodly, without even having received the churches' input, accountability, or correction from fellow elders at his own church or churches all over the world? **"Every good gift and every perfect gift is from above, and cometh down from the Father of lights, with whom is no variableness, neither shadow of turning."**[130]

Christians certainly can use the word peace. However, to claim a blueprint is directly from God when it can easily be confused with a New Ager's global peace plan raises a concern. God is not the author of confusion; a clear and *distinct* signal would be sent by him:

> For if the trumpet give an uncertain sound, who shall prepare himself to the battle?[131]

> For God is not the author of confusion, but of peace, as in all churches of the saints.[132]

If Rick Warren's PEACE plan is really inspired from God as he claims, it should already arrive perfect. It wouldn't need perfecting! Furthermore, Jesus Christ's global peace plan is inaugurated at His return, not before. When it begins, there will be no wicked

---

129   Ibid.

130   James 1:17

131   1 Corinthians 14:8

132   1 Corinthians 14:33

on the earth, only mortal believers and immortal glorified saints, for He will have destroyed the wicked, the Antichrist (and his peace plan), and bound Satan! "There is no peace, saith my God, to the wicked."[133]

---

133   Isaiah 57:21

Chapter 9

Purpose-Driven Country

Rick Warren had been talking to world leaders over the last year, getting their opinions and factoring them into his five-step PEACE plan.[134] He recruits soldiers from the enemy camp, or promotes them, or votes for the enemy camp, including those who endorse Rick Warren's teachings:

What follows is an account of some of the principal leaders working with or directly for Rick Warren, presently implementing his global PEACE plan. What follows should help give you great insight into how Rick Warren is transforming Africa into a purpose-driven continent, as well as the rest of the world with his revisionist Christianity!

How Rick Warren Is Masquerading as an Angel of Light Transforming Your Church and Country

Upon receiving many e-mails around the world from concerned Christians that their church or country is being taking over or "transformed" by Rick Warren's purpose-driven church model and his global PEACE plan, and others asking me how one knows their own church has become purpose-driven, I felt compelled to write this article in response to these SOS calls for help. There is a recent article posted on this very transformation and how

---

134   Warren Smith, *Deceived on Purpose*, p. 127.

to identify it, entitled "Are you in the throes of Transformation?"[135]

The article was so brilliant, I decided that it would be very constructive to the body of Christ to build on that very theme, as well as clear up a lot of confusion. What follows is both an update and a case study of how Rick Warren is taking over churches and countries. One of the main presentations of Warren's Saddleback Church staff was given by Todd Hudnall, who was senior pastor of the First Assembly of God Church (see Appendix C) in San Diego, California (on March 27, 2006, he became pastor of Radiant Church in Colorado Springs), and was also a featured speaker at the Purpose Driven conference in Florida in April 2006.[136]

Following are excerpts from the conference in Kenya:

Todd Hudnall, Sr. Pastor, First Assembly of God of San Diego*
Presentation of Rick Warren's PDC to Nairobi Pentecostal Church
Nairobi, Kenya — November 8–11, 2005
with Commentary by James Sundquist
and Contributing Editor and Commentary by Pastor Bob DeWaay

TODD HUDNALL on behalf of Rick Warren . . .

The message we are sharing you could call an operating system for the church. Without the Intel chip, the computer would not work. I believe that the Purpose Driven Church model is a processing chip for the church of Jesus Christ. I believe it works whether it is in San Diego, California, or Kenya, Africa. It works because it is God's purpose. **It is God's plan.**

---

135 herescope.blogspot.com/

136 www.purposedriven.com/en-US/Events/PurposeDrivenPentecostalCharismatic-LakeForestCA/Uncompromised_speakers.htm

. . . And what God has done through Dr. Rick Warren is provide a model which we can fulfill those purposes and become the prevailing church that God wants us to be. . . . This message is very biblical.

RESPONSE

Well this message is very much *not* biblical. The operating system for the church is not an object. It is a Person — the Person of Jesus Christ and the Person of the Holy Spirit (who will lead you in all truth). Jesus Christ is the author and finisher of our salvation whether in the first century or the twenty-first century. Jesus did not say that apart from a computer chip you cannot operate; He said "apart from *me* you can do nothing!" So the premise of Hudnall and Warren is fatally flawed. And even if the operating system for the church is an Intel chip, computers didn't even exist in the church for nineteen hundred years. So how did the church function all of these years without this chip? How did the church function before this chip? According to so-called "post-moderns" and PDCers, it didn't. The old model (the biblical "preaching Jesus Christ," repentance, being born again, warning of coming judgment, Hell) is a dismal failure. What audacity to proclaim that Rick Warren's method holds the key that throughout the ages the church has missed. Maybe this is why they are so intent on rewriting the Bible and promoting perverse translations of it!

At the end of this conference Hudnall changed the definition from "a processing chip" to *the* processing chip or model for the twenty-first century church. This boastful statement means that every church which does not have Rick Warren's purpose-driven model is outside of God's plan. If you don't go along with it, they claim they will try to help you find another church you are happy with. But why would you want to do that, if in so doing you would in effect be *outside* of God's plan? There are a great number of accounts in which there is not even another local church to send people to because all the surrounding churches too have become purpose-driven. And even if the analogy of the Intel chip were true—that the operating system for the church must be run by this chip—then the chip is defective because it would recognize that the model would not work in a computer which was a synagogue or Roman Catholic church because these are another gospel. This operating system which they claim "is God's plan" fails to recognize the apostle Paul's own words that "I have not failed to give you the *whole* counsel of God." Apparently not, since Paul forgot to supply us with the counsel of Warren's purpose-driven model.

PASTOR BOB DEWAAY'S COMMENTS:

1. Pastor Hudnall makes a very bold claim—that Rick Warren has invented a new operating system for the church. With computers, the operating system is the most essential part of the computer. Take out the CPU chip and the computer is dead and worthless. Can we believe that the church itself is dead and worthless without Warren's plan?

2. How can a program (PDC) not invented until the twentieth century have such a key role? Without the operating system, the computer is dead. Does this mean every church that existed since the day of Pentecost was dead? If not, then evidently these churches had something analogous to an operating system before. So what was the previous operating system that is being removed and replaced with the PDC one? The speech in question does not tell us what that old CPU was that has to go. If they cannot answer these questions, their claims should be dismissed.

3. Biblically what is most analogous to an operating system in a computer is Jesus Christ as the head of the church and the Holy Spirit as the life of the church. Either the PDC is removing these to replace them with the new processor, or

the PDC is not really a new operating system and they are making a false claim to say that it is.

4. The speech in question uses the terms "God's plan" and "purpose-driven" synonymously. In logic this is called "begging the question." Why should we have to accept the idea the purpose-driven model is indeed God's plan before we have heard any evidence that it is? They claim too much for a man-made program.

5. They would have to admit that the purpose-driven model did not exist during the New Testament. It is up to them to prove that what they are doing is able to improve on the teachings and practices of the New Testament, without compromising them. They fail to prove this and there is much evidence that they do compromise those teachings.

TODD HUDNALL:

. . . Back in 1992 I became acquainted with Dr. Warren and his Saddleback model for the Purpose Driven Churches, and heard what God was doing at Saddleback. At that time I was looking for answers. And when I saw this model, I said this is God's plan. This allows us to fulfill what God wants us to fulfill for his church.

So I brought this model to our church and we begin to see immediate church growth, of consistently seeing 20 percent growth every year. Let me say that percentage is a good percentage. When you get much faster than 20 percent it is difficult to keep up with the growth. You can do it. But it becomes very difficult. Signs and wonders and miracles begin to happen.

I have seen revival, but I have seen revivals actually damages churches over time because they lose their focus, they lose their purpose. They begin to see the move of God as something for them . . . **to help them fulfill their agenda.**

RESPONSE:
The fact remains that Rick Warren does have an agenda, that is his personal blueprint for the earth.

PASTOR BOB DEWAAY'S COMMENTS:
Again the speaker (Hudnall) is begging the question. That he *thinks/thought* that it is God's plan does not prove that it is. That his church grew and there were signs and wonders does not prove this was from God. False religions grow and have signs and wonders. What he does not prove is that the purpose-driven model is taught in the New Testament. He is appealing to personal experience rather than scripture. We need to consult the Bible for the appropriate agenda.

TODD HUDNALL:
> I believe God wants to bring a revival to Kenya, but there needs to be a way to handle it. You cannot pour new wine into old wineskins. We've got to have a **wineskin** that the Holy Spirit can use . . . that can contain the revival that God wants to bring. So I believe that the Purpose Driven model is such a wineskin.

RESPONSE:
Once again, Warren's PDC program redefines the scriptural meaning of words. The old wineskins referred to by Jesus Christ himself were the old covenant and the traditions of the scribes and Pharisees (the religious leaders in Israel). The new wineskins in Scripture refer to the new covenant. There is no replacing the new covenant. According to Hudnall's logic, the church which functions as the new covenant must be replaced by another new covenant or new wineskin.

Rick Warren has convinced millions of people that the church must be transformed. Warren's reformation reverses the First Reformation and insults the church at large, which has been persecuted and martyred throughout this present age which somehow mistakenly thought it was carrying out the "deeds" of the new covenant. Rick Warren has usurped the authorship of the new wineskin.

The purpose-driven church is a man-made invention of Rick Warren. Therefore, it is impossible that it could be a new wineskin. The church does not need a wineskin that the Holy Spirit can use (as though until Rick Warren came along, it did not already have wineskins that the Holy Spirit could use since the foundation of the church)! In fact, in reality Hudnall and Warren have replaced the new covenant (new wineskin) with much of the *same* old wineskin of the old covenant and traditions of men, putting unnecessary burdens on Christians and stealing away their liberty in Christ.

Rick Warren and Todd Hudnall need to read the seven woes that Christ laid on the Pharisees and scribes,[137] as well as the first chapter of Galatians before they continue to put Christians right back under bondage. The old wineskin was rabbinic Judaism and the old covenant practices. The new wineskin is messianic salvation and the church built on the rock that the gates of Hell will not prevail against. What the gates of Hell can't prevail against does not need replacing. Judaism as it was would not be able to hold what God was doing such as in Acts.

The claim that some man-made movement that did not exist until the twentieth century is what Jesus meant by "new wineskins" is indefensible biblically. The new wineskin has existed since Pentecost and it will never become the "old wineskin" until Jesus returns. This shows that bad theology and bad biblical exegesis are common practices in the PDC.

---

137   See Matthew 23:13–29

TODD HUDNALL:

You are to reach that community and bring the community in to become part of the crowd, then after they become part of the crowd, . . . you bring them and make them be part of your congregation. Then they become committed in growing in Christ. Finally they become your core people for ministry . . . turning them into an army, making them part of your core . . . your center.

RESPONSE:

This model is found nowhere in Scripture and in fact is backwards regarding the order. Seek ye *first* the kingdom of God. Seek the light (His Word) and He will supply the fellowship or community.

PASTOR BOB DEWAAY'S COMMENTS:

This is the fundamental error of the seeker movement. The Lord adds people to the church through saving them.[138] The "crowd" is outside of the church and should be the subject of gospel preaching, not trying to change the church to make it attractive to the unregenerate mind.

TODD HUDNALL:

BUILDING YOUR CONGREGATION . . . (Outer Circle)
Concept of membership is very biblical. It is taught all the way through the New Testament.

In 1 Corinthians 12, it tells us that the Holy Spirit takes us when we receive Jesus Christ and plunges us into the Body of Christ. . . . In 1 Corinthian 13 . . . you may be eyes, you may be ears you may be nose. . . .

---

138   See Acts 2:47

"Saul, Saul, why do you persecute me." Saul could have said, "I'm not persecuting you, I'm persecuting the church." Jesus is saying if you persecute the church you are persecuting the body and that is me. . . . We need to belong to the church family. Ephesian 2:19 says this: "Now you are no longer strangers to God and foreigners to Heaven, but you are members of God's very own family." And you belong to God's household with every other Christian. Notice we are members of his Body. Membership is biblical. Romans 12:5 says this: "In Christ, we who are many form one body, and each member belongs to all the others."

Now it is important that we explain the benefits of membership, the value of membership, and the importance of membership. So when people come to your church you want to let them know that they can become a member. And when people join, it gives them significance, it gives them meaning, it gives them purpose, it gives them connection and it gives them community. . . . Church membership is really a step of spiritual maturity. . . . How you do it is you create a climate where people want to join.

Now there are two things that people crave most. People want love and people want acceptance. All of us want that. We were designed to desire that. We want to be loved and accepted; *we* crave that. . . . And those are the two things that Jesus commanded us to demonstrate. In John 13:35, Jesus said this: "By this you shall all men know that you are my disciples that you love one another." The church is to show people that come to it love! Romans 15:7 says, "accept one another just as Christ has accepted you." We are to accept people that come in to our church just as Jesus accepted us. . . .

Now in America there is a stereotype some have of the church of it being judgmental, of it being critical, of it being condemning. The church should never have that kind of reputation. The church should be loving and accepting to people. Now here is a fact you need to know: *"Growing churches love, and loving churches grow."*

RESPONSE:
Read God's Word. We are called to love, yet God is judgmental, critical, and condemning to those who are in rebellion, not born again, living according to their own plans. Biblical churches might shrink! The Mormon Church is loving and the Mormon Church is growing.

PASTOR BOB DEWAAY'S COMMENTS:
Again there is a purposeful erasing the boundary between the church and the world. He fails to distinguish between membership in a 501(c)3 corporation (local organization that people join) and membership in the body of Christ which happens through conversion. The passages he cites have to do with the type of relationships true believers have with one another. But in the PDC model, they integrate the regenerate and unregenerate and confuse the unity of the corporation with the true unity through the gospel that true believers have. That God is loving is true. That we should be loving is true. But for the unregenerate to be converted, they must be convinced they are law breakers abiding under God's wrath unless they repent. Telling them these truths is loving. The idea that we will "woo" sinners into the church by being nice people—all the while failing to tell them of the peril they are in as sinners—is not biblical.

TODD HUDNALL:
Church growth expert Winn Arn [founder of American Institute of Church Growth, now Church Growth] . . . did a study of 10,000 church members all over America and rated them according to friendliness. And after he did the rating, he found

that in every single denomination, the friendliest, they were the fastest growing. And those that weren't considered friendly, weren't growing. . . . And if you want people to be a part of your church, you have to create a climate of love and acceptance. Now the single most important factor that causes people to stay in your churches is relationships. . . . People will come to your church for all kinds of reasons, but they stay in their church because of relationships. . . . **Now the Bible refers to biblical relationships by a word, and that word is fellowship.**

RESPONSE:

The Bible also says: "And have no fellowship with the unfruitful works of darkness, but rather reprove them" (Eph. 5:11).

PASTOR BOB DEWAAY'S COMMENTS:

I wonder how "friendly" they would consider Stephen:

Ye stiffnecked and uncircumcised in heart and ears, ye do always resist the Holy Ghost: as your fathers did, so do ye. Which of the prophets have not your fathers persecuted? and they have slain them which shewed before of the coming of the Just One; of whom ye have been now the betrayers and murderers: Who have received the law by the disposition of angels, and have not kept it.[139]

Again, they make the same error over and over: trying to "woo" the unregenerate by making the church look appealing to them in their lost state rather than preaching for conversions.

TODD HUDNALL:

And there is a lot of myths about fellowship. . . . Small churches

---

139   Acts 7:51–53

are friendly and large churches are cold and impersonal. And that's not true. . . . Small churches can turn into a clique. You know what cliques are? They won't let others in. . . . Actually often large churches are more accepting, because the only way you are going to grow bigger is by caring about individuals, not by caring about crowds. . . . An impersonal church will not grow. The largest church in the world today is in Seoul Korea. . . . It is a church of around 750,000 people. . . .

RESPONSE:
He is referring to Paul (David) Yonggi Cho's church. Is this a good example of a Christian leader? What Hudnall failed to tell you is who the pastor of this church is and what he teaches. Let us see what this man teaches:

Similar to Rick Warren's SHAPE program, Rev. Cho's Fourth Dimension theology is based on occultist Carl Jung. "Cho's mystical foundation is built upon the sands of *Sigmund Freud's* and *Carl Jung's subconscious mind* rather than the rock of Jesus Christ."[140] For more on the true teachings of David Cho, I invite you to read: "Occult Healing Builds World's Largest Church: The Influence of Paul Yonggi Cho."[141]

PASTOR BOB DEWAAY'S COMMENTS:
Agreed, Cho is a heretic and if he is an example of anything, it is the example of compromising the gospel to gain the approval of men.

HUDNALL:
We have to have our churches organized in such a way that

---

140 www.rapidnet.com/~jbeard/bdm/exposes/cho/general.htm—see also 1 Cor. 3:11

141 wayoflife.org/fbns/occulthealing.htm

we create a climate of love and acceptance. . . . At Saddleback Church . . . every first time visitor we give "first impressions" card. . . . "Our church wants to serve you better. **Would you please give us your opinion."** We ask three questions: this is what I notice first, this is what I like best, this is what I like least. Let me give you some reactions of cards at Saddleback Church: . . . "people were warm and friendly," "they were friendly people," "I feel warm and comfortable and at ease," "there was a warm and loving atmosphere," "I felt comfortable and happy.". . . The church is an organization that is built for the benefit of non-members to see them become members.

RESPONSE:

This is just one more example of the error in Warren's teachings — more Robert Schuller and Bill Hybels. Opinions, opinions, and still more opinions, looking for the " I feel warm and comfortable and at ease" response. Opinions were never the foundation of the true churches built throughout the church age. How about hearing a truly anointed, Holy Ghost-breathed sermon? Where sinners cringe under the mighty hand of God and whose hearts fail them because of the dread of the Lord and His coming wrath? Where they fall on their faces before the living God or run to the altar to repent and be saved? The preaching of God's Word is convicting!! That is the work of the Holy Spirit! To convict — it is *not* to make us feel comfortable in our sin!! Hudnall is advocating building a community in direct conflict with the true work of the Holy Spirit. The world will be offended at the preaching of Jesus, the true gospel. They will be extremely uncomfortable and hate it. So the Bible tells us, again and again.

The church is not built for non-members. It is built for believers to be trained up in righteousness and the instruction of the doctrines of the apostles. It is a place for believers to love and encourage one another. Certainly non-members will benefit if they repent, but it holds virtually nothing for them as non–believers unless they are hearing the Word of God. We already have the Rotary Club and many other wonderful organizations that offer community and good deeds. Once again, this is upside down, backward theology which is paving the way to Kingdom Now theology.

PASTOR BOB DEWAAY'S COMMENT:
Agreed: "Woe unto you when all men speak well of you."

HUDNALL:
We have a three minute rule. . . . You have to greet people you don't know. . . . One of the greatest needs people have is for friendliness, there is a need for that. The church must provide friendliness. People aren't just looking for a friendly church, they're looking for friends. **They're looking for relationships.**

RESPONSE:
Is this "friendship" the focus of the Bible? Does this even remotely resemble the teaching of the prophets, Jesus, the disciples? I could address this further, but Paul Proctor has already written one of the best articles, which should help demolish this stronghold, entitled "Religious Relativism."[142]

PASTOR BOB DEWAAY'S COMMENTS:
Agreed; this is the same error repeated over and over — we have to give the unregenerate what they are looking for. The Bible tells us what they are looking for: "Among whom also we all had our conversation in times past in the lusts of our flesh, fulfilling the desires of the flesh and of the mind; and were by nature the

---

142 www.newswithviews.com/PaulProctor/proctor50.htm

children of wrath, even as others."[143] What they want is not just friendship; but they want self-fulfillment in this world without submitting to God on His terms.

TODD HUDNALL:

> Now I want to say some things that are not in the notes. . . . I particularly want to talk to the pastors who are here. . . . How do you develop a caring congregation. Well let me tell you, it always starts with leadership. . . . **One the greatest things you can do to help your church grow pastor, is to smile.**

RESPONSE:

I should remind the reader that equipping leaders is the "E" in Rick Warren's global PEACE plan. (See Appendix A on John Maxwell and the principles behind his leadership training.) Just "put on a happy face," right? I can certainly imagine Hananiah the false prophet smiling while he told the Israelites only good things are going to happen to them.[144] We know that Jeremiah wasn't smiling; Scripture only records his great anguish. In fact there is whole book by Jeremiah entitled *Lamentations*. So you can follow the smile, or you can follow the truth that Jeremiah preached. Were David, Paul, and Jesus — all of whom despaired unto death — smiling in this despair? The book of Habakkuk is devoted to this prophets *complaints*. So shouldn't he have not complained to his congregation so he could recruit more followers and so his congregation would grow?

TODD HUDNALL:

> There is nothing worse than a sad, sour, frowning pastor.

---

143   Ephesians 2:3

144   See Jeremiah 28:15-16

RESPONSE:

Actually there are many things worse than a sad, sour, frowning pastor . . . such as a smiling pastor like Robert Schuller who is false teacher of the highest order, leading multitudes astray. And Rick Warren is usually smiling, and his teachings are all riddled with falsehood. I would much rather listen to the sad and frowning Jeremiah or Habbakuk than to a smiling false teacher. And even a true teacher may often need to be sad, as Paul was with bitter tears and tearing his robes as he watched false teaching come into the early church. A pastor should be sad when there is sin in the body of Christ.

A smiling pastor proves nothing. Here are accounts of flattering speech in the Old Testament. I am quite certain these enticements to sin were not "sad, sour, or frowning":

> Let me not, I pray you, accept any man's person, neither let me give **flattering** titles unto man. For I know not to give **flattering** titles; in so doing my maker would soon take me away.[145]

> They speak vanity every one with his neighbour: with flattering lips and with a double heart do they speak. The LORD shall cut off all **flattering lips**, and the tongue that speaketh proud things.[146]

> With her much fair speech she caused him to yield, with the **flattering of her lips** she forced him.[147]

> A lying tongue hateth those that are afflicted by it; and a **flattering mouth** worketh ruin.[148]

---

145 Job 32:21–22

146 Psalm 12:2–3

147 Proverbs 7:21

148 Proverbs 26:28

Which say to the seers, See not; and to the prophets, Proph-esy not unto us right things, **speak unto us smooth things**, prophesy deceits.[149]

For there shall be no more any vain vision nor **flattering divi-nation** within the house of Israel.[150]

And regarding people being led astray with smiles on their faces, we read:

The prophets prophesy falsely, and the priests bear rule by their means; **and my people love to have it so:** and what will ye do in the end thereof?[151]

And how does Hudnall think seducing spirits described by Paul are going to appear? With *"nothing worse than a sad, sour, frowning"*? Are Satan's servants masquerading as servants of righteousness going to come across with *"nothing worse than a sad, sour, frowning"*? Here are but three New Testament scriptures to refute Hudnall's false premise:

For false Christs and false prophets shall rise, and shall shew signs and wonders, to seduce, if it were possible, even the elect. But take ye heed: behold, I have foretold you all things.[152]

. . . by **good word and fair speeches** deceive the heart of the simple.[153]

---

149   Isaiah 30:10

150   Ezekiel 12:24

151   Jeremiah 5:31

152   Mark 13:22–23

153   Romans 16:18

For neither at any time used we flattering words, as ye know, nor a cloke of covetousness; God is witness.[154]

TODD HUDNALL:

. . . If you want to know the temperature of your church, how warm your church is, the first thing you have to do is stick a thermometer in your mouth. Because as goes the leader, so goes the church. . . . You've got to work at being friendly. . . . Personally I am a little bit of an introvert . . . so I've had to force myself to get out of my comfort zone and reach out . . . and be loving and be friendly. . . . Be approachable, be real. . . . We have to continue to develop warmth and integrity and people skills. There are many good books actually that can help you. I know many of you are familiar with John Maxwell. He has written many books about people skills. There is a book very famous in America, and I think around the world by Dale Carnegie, it is called "How To Win Friends and Influence People." It is not a Christian book

RESPONSE:

John Maxwell is the chairman of Pastors Global Network. Maxwell is setting up an international pastoral accrediting association which will credential pastors, re-train them, and yes, more measuring to see who will fit the new criteria. One has to wonder what will happen to those pastors who don't meet Maxwell's standards or measure up to his criteria or meet his outcome-based Christianity performance standards. Maxwell is also the head the "Million Leader Mandate" (mandated by whom?) which is part of International Church Ministries (Dr. Phil Walker). I recently listened to one of the last tapes on that conference in Nairobi.

---

154   1 Thessalonians 2:5

John Jackson, one of the main speakers, even confirmed that they are using the Million Leader Mandate in their PDC programs as well as Transitions (Dan Sutherland).

So there is no more mystery. It is now confirmed. They are all a gang of thieves—stealing the Lord's church. And if any doubt remains how much John Maxwell is at the core of Rick Warren's global PEACE plan, **the first "E" in Warren's PEACE acronym stand for EQUIP**, a non-profit organization founded by Dr. John Maxwell, where he is partnered with still another false teacher: Joyce Meyers. These ministries don't even attempt to disguise the fact that they are ecumenical, which you can verify by simply visiting their websites.

John Maxwell is also the president of Injoy Ministries, which he began in San Diego and moved to Atlanta, Georgia, in 1997. For many years he was pastor of Skyline Wesleyan Church in La Mesa (greater San Diego), California. His website is www.injoy. com. Maxwell was one of the speakers at the summer 2005 Willowcreek Summit with Rick Warren.

John Maxwell's books are not good books! (For more extensive information on John Maxwell, see Appendix A). John Maxwell wrote the foreword for John Jackson's book *Pastorpreneur*, the other major speaker at this same purpose-driven church conference.

John Jackson is also a promoter of apostate Dr. Robert Schuller.[155] I recently corresponded with Kevin Trevithick who is in charge of Warren's SHAPE (301 Class) program at Pastor John Jackson's church, Carson Valley Christian Church in Nevada.[156] I had written him an appeal to reconsider presenting this Jung-based personality temperament divination to his members. In an e-mail dated March 17, 2006, Trevithick responded with defend-

---

155   www.pastorpreneur.com/pp_impact5.html

156   www.carsonvalleychristian.com

ing his extensive theology training (at Fuller) and stated: "I prefer associations with those who focus on what they are *for*, rather than what they are *against*." This is rather a startling response in light of the fact that eight of the Ten Commandments are comprised of what God is "against," and a great deal of Scripture is devoted to what God is "against."

Upon visiting Carson Valley Christian Church's website, I discovered that Rick Warren's temperament divination was not the only magic arts programs being run there. They also conduct martial arts classes. If you think this is a good Christian practice at a church, I invite you to read Rev. Ed Hird's article, "Taekwondo and the Martial Arts: Mere Exercise or Trojan Horse??"[157] as well as Linda Nathan's article entitled "Karate, Kids, and the Culture: Your Child and the Martial Arts."[158] This is in stark contrast to what the Christians in the early church did in the book of Acts where they burned magic arts books vs. promoting them.

Even the third speaker, Dr. Phil Walker (of the three major speakers listed on program as Rick Warren's staff), touted John Maxwell. It should be pointed out that Hudnall, Jackson, and Walker were not simply independent speakers who just happened to show up and be speakers at the same event. Walker introduced both Hudnall and Jackson, emphasizing how critical their message was to the purpose-driven model. Jackson in turn also spoke of the urgency of Todd Hudnall's purpose-driven essential components and the importance of hearing his presentations. All three promoted Maxwell. The bottom line is that they all reinforce each other. And all three are major key global players and speakers for Rick Warren's PDC agenda!

Phil Walker is the president of International Christian Min-

---

157 www3.telus.net/st_simons/arm07.htm
www.canadianchristianity.com/cgi-bin/bc.cgi?bc/bccn/0902/artidolatrous

158 www.crossroad.to/articles2/05/karate.htm

istries, where he also promotes John Maxwell. His organization (ICM) has also formed a partnership/unholy alliance with Dr. Ralph Winter's organization, U.S. Center for World Mission, including its dominionist curriculum entitled "Perspectives." If there remains any doubt that Ralph Winter is a false teacher, I invite you to read the documentation that corroborates it.[159] I refer you to Sarah Leslie's excellent speech on how Fullerton and the PDC have hijacked the church.[160] Regarding Ralph Winter, I also invite you to read Al Dager's *Media Spotlight* article, "The World Christian Movement."[161]

The website for International Christian Ministries[162] says that ICM coordinates the programs of purpose-driven ministries in Africa and the Middle East. ICM has also formed a direct alliance with John Maxwell from their website:

> ICM has agreed to represent John Maxwell's Million Leader Mandate in Africa. The goal of this program is to see over 300,000 leaders go through six courses developed by Equip. This program is scheduled to run through 2008.

Phil Walker is a major global player in Warren's worldwide purpose-driven schematic who was responsible for setting up this conference in Nairobi, as well as spearheading five seminaries and conferences in twenty-four countries, putting on two hundred conferences a year. So it is impossible to dismiss the magnitude of John Maxwell's role and impact in Warren's purpose-driven church campaign. Here is John Maxwell's endorsement of John Jackson's book:

---

159   http://watch.pair.com/fuller.html

160   www.pinebrook-aog.com/conference.htm

161   www.intotruth.org/globalism/WCM3.html

162   www.icmusa.org/partnerships/php

If you're thinking your way through developing a new church
or being an agent for change in your present ministry, *Pastorpreneur* is worth reading. John Jackson knows what he's talking
about because he's lived it. . . .

—from the foreword by John Maxwell[163]

Upon visiting his own personal website as well as his church's
website, I find that he too promotes John Maxwell's books as
valuable resources, as well as Mormon author and New Age
promoter Stephen Covey (Carson Valley Christian Center in
Minden, Nevada[164] and president of VisionQuest Ministries[165]).

Dale Carnegie. What is Hudnall doing promoting the book
of someone who is not a Christian to a conference of pastors and
Christians? Hudnall quotes the Scripture in this purpose-driven
church conference that the natural man understands not the
things of the spirit, yet he goes ahead and promotes the natural
man Dale Carnegie, who is not a Christian. The title alone from
his book, *How to Win Friends and Influence People,* should be a red
flag to Christians and particularly to pastors like Hudnall. Hudnall should have said to this congregation regarding Carnegie's
title and teaching:

Ye adulterers and adulteresses, know ye not that the **friendship
of the world is enmity with God?** whosoever therefore will be
a **friend of the world is the enemy of God.**[166]

Hudnall also seems to forget, "Blessed is that man that maketh
the LORD his trust, and respecteth not the proud, nor such as turn

---

163   www.pastorpreneur.com/reviews.html

164   www.drjohnjackson.com/who.html

165   www.carsonvalleychristian.com

166   James 4:4

aside to lies."[167] Dale Carnegie, a non-believer, tells us how to win friends and influence people, while Scripture tells us that friendship with the world is enmity with God.

TODD HUDNALL:

But it has very good principles about how to be loving and how to be friendly toward people. Now let me give you some ideas on how to show you are approachable towards people. . . . People, "why did you come to Saddleback and why did you come back?" People will see what they like about the church . . . the positives. Next explain to them the *baseball diamond*. . . .

RESPONSE:

Yes, please do explain to us the *baseball diamond*. I discuss Rick Warren's baseball diamond in Appendix B. Warren's Discovery Classes (his baseball diamond) 101–401 have little to do with salvation and sanctification or Christian theology but are about taking oaths to commit one's self to serving a PDC.

TODD HUDNALL:

Here is a letter that Pastor Rick received from someone who visited his church and visited his house. They said: "Pastor Rick is just a real person, like I am. I feel that he would like me just as much as I liked him." This is an attitude you can even develop. Let me tell you a place you can develop this, pastors. It is in your pulpit. When you are real, people know that you have struggles. You too have challenges . . . just be honest about it. . . . That's one of the things about God. He became a man so that he could become approachable in the person of Jesus. . . .

---

167   Psalm 40:4

RESPONSE:

And where is this doctrine taught in Scripture? Jesus came to pay the penalty for sin and to appease his Father's wrath! Having done this, Jesus Christ is not more approachable . . . in fact, He is a rock of offense, despised and rejected and we esteemed Him *not*. See Psalm 22 and Isaiah 53, as well as the following verses.

> As it is written, Behold, I lay in Sion a stumblingstone and rock of offence: and whosoever believeth on him shall not be ashamed.[168]

> And a stone of stumbling, and a rock of offence, even to them which stumble at the word, being disobedient: whereunto also they were appointed.[169]

PASTOR BOB DEWAAY'S COMMENTS:

Saying Jesus became a man to become more approachable so we should therefore make ourselves approachable is a misrepresentation of the purpose of the incarnation. It merely makes Jesus a "good example to follow" rather than the unique One who provided a substitutionary atonement.

TODD HUDNALL:

Dale Carnegie said: "There is no sweeter word in any language than a person's name to them."

RESPONSE:

Of course if you're trying to build a business, knowing the names of your customers is very important. It is universal that we all

---

168   Romans 9:33

169   1 Peter 2:8

appreciate having people in the church know our names. But from a biblical perspective, hearing our name is sweet depending on whether we are guilty or not! If hearing the voice of the Lord calling out to them was so sweet to the hearing, then why did Adam and Eve hide and cover their nakedness? God called out Cain's name after he murdered his brother. Was Cain's name being called sweet for Cain to hear? Saul called out Samuel's name in the account of the witch of Endor. Did Samuel think that was sweet music to his hears? No, he was very upset at being disturbed from the grave when Saul practiced divination. And Abraham, Jacob, and Saul in the book of Acts all had their names changed, so their new name would have been much sweeter because the Lord changed their names.

And this is now the second time we hear Hudnall recommending the counsel of Dale Carnegie, a non-believer. The sweetest word in any language should not be my own name, rather it should be the name of Jesus Christ, the Rose of Sharon.

TODD HUDNALL:

Actually, scientists tell us that by not being touched enough can have skin deprivation. True, we need to be touched. . . .

RESPONSE:

Is "touchy-feely" the proper focus of the church?

TODD HUDNALL:

Why don't you say that with me: "Give them a look, give them a word, and give them touch." . . . Here is a copy of a note that Pastor Rick Warren received from one of the people of his church. It said: "Pastor Rick, I can't tell you what it meant to me when on Friday, you put your arms around me in comfort.

It felt as though Jesus' arms were holding me in such compassion and tenderness. I know now that I will make it through this not so exciting time. And I know he sent me here so I could feel God's caring love." . . . Here is another note he received, . . . "Thanks for making me feel special." . . . Here is another thing, use humor. . . . If you make jokes about yourself, you will always have a lot to joke about. . . .

Each of us have to make a decision. Are we going to impress people or are we going to influence people. Because you can't do both. You can impress people from a distance, but you influence them up close. . . . We have to get close to people if we want to influence them.

RESPONSE:

The apostle Paul spent most of his time a great distance from the churches he started and those he simply wrote to in his letters. He had great influence on them at a distance, as well as up close. And he instructed his epistles to be read and circulated to other Christians and churches, many of which were far away in time and distance. In fact his influence throughout the church age is far more extensive than any he saw or touched up close. Jesus Christ in fact even rebuked Thomas for having to "touch" his wounds while commending those who believed and obeyed who never even saw Jesus' face while he was on the earth—all Christians since the first century, and the rest of us who are Christians living in the twenty-first century. I am in many ways more influenced by brothers and sisters around the world that I correspond with that I may never meet until the wedding supper of the Lamb. Conversely, I know many people that I am up close to in which I have no influence and they have none on me. Using geographic distance as a formula or litmus test is at best precarious and can be shot full of holes simply by observing New Testament accounts of church life.

PASTOR BOB DEWAAYS COMMENTS:

I would say that Hudnall creates a false dilemma — either influence or impress. We are not seeking to do either; we are seeking to be faithful to God through gospel preaching so that He, by His grace, will convert them. Whether they are influenced or impressed with us personally is of little concern. The power is through the Holy Spirit convicting.

TODD HUDNALL:

Healthy churches have pastors who are not afraid to get up close to people. Accept and affirm diversity among your members. Healthy churches focus on unity, on uniformity. . . .

Now the thing that we don't want to do is use guilt to motivate people. Because that is not accepting. You see, here is the reason a lot of us use guilt to motivate people. Because it works. But it is not healthy. And over the long term it is going to be damaging.

RESPONSE:

This notion is patently absurd. All of the prophets of the Old Testament laid a guilt trip on the people, whether Noah, Jonah, Jeremiah, etc. Guilt is good if you are guilty — that means you are convicted of sin. The preaching of repentance in both testaments was to point out their guilt. Over the long term it is damaging if you refrain from teaching them they are guilty, as "all have sinned and come short of the glory of God." Guilt motivates people to repent. So do you think they are going to repent if they think they aren't guilty, if faith cometh by hearing — but they never hear that they are guilty, as Warren tragically does in his *Ladies Home Journal* column?

As to what is "healthy," the healthiest thing that Nathan the prophet could have done to David was to tell him he was guilty in his adultery with Bathsheba. David was motivated to repent! Pastor Bob DeWaay demolishes this stronghold of false teaching about a healthy church in his book *Redefining Christianity*. As a pastor, you better worry if your congregation is not motivated by guilt. People with reprobate minds whose consciences have been seared like a hot iron are not motivated by guilt. This is the *final* stage of apostasy and could not be more *unhealthy*. The Scriptures warn us about this state of mind. Christians everywhere should be thankful to the Lord that they still have the ability to feel guilty — it is a great and righteous motivator!!!

PASTOR BOB DEWAAY COMMENTS:
The biblical pattern is to preach the law that shows people their own guilt before God and preach the gospel so they see the only hope for escape. We are not motivating them to serve us, but to turn to God and receive the free gift of salvation. Hudnall doesn't make it clear about motivation to do what, so it makes the issue muddy.

TODD HUDNALL:
We have a membership class in our church. And some issues that we teach are personal preferences and personal convictions are up to the individual. . . . I shouldn't judge him over his convictions and he shouldn't judge me over my convictions. . . . Preach the word, live your convictions. Don't preach your convictions. And in your church, if you want to be an accepting church, you have to accept the fact that you can't push convictions on people. Everyone has to live their own convictions. . . . Understand that we live in a time when people mainly don't choose a church because of its denomination. They choose a church that meets their need.

Romans 14:19 says this: "Let us concentrate on the things

that make for harmony and the growth of our fellowship together."

RESPONSE:

He uses the PH translation. Let us Compare this verse to KVJ:

Let us therefore follow after the things which make for peace, and things wherewith one may edify another.

Note there is nothing in there about church growth! In fact there is nothing in Scripture that gives us a mandate to grow the church or commandments to do so!

TODD HUDNALL:

Augustine said this: "In essentials we have unity, in non-essentials we have liberty, and in all things we show charity."

RESPONSE:

This famous motto of Christian Irenics, which I have slightly modified in the text, is often falsely attributed to St. Augustin (whose creed would not allow it, though his heart might have approved of it), but is of much later origin. It appears for the first time in Germany, A.D. 1627 and 1628, among peaceful divines of the Lutheran and German Reformed churches, and found hearty welcome among moderate divines In England.[170]

TODD HUDNALL:

You see there are some essentials. You have to believe that salvation comes through faith alone in Christ alone. . . .

---

170   www.ccel.org/ccel/schaff/hcc7.ii.vii.viii.html

RESPONSE:
Yes, the doctrine of salvation through faith alone is essential (as this is what the Reformation was about). Countless Christians could have saved themselves from being burned at the stake by simply denying this *Sola Scriptura* doctrine. It is curious that Rick Warren is forming an unholy alliance with the Roman Catholic Church for his purpose-driven programs when the Roman Catholic Church put forth in the Council of Trent that those Protestants who hold such views are anathematized (cursed).

TODD HUDNALL:
Now if you will do some of these things as a leader and you treat people with love and acceptance, you'll have no problem in getting people to come to your church.

Communicate the value of membership. . . . What membership should be is not conformity, but commitment. . . . That is the difference between someone who just attends your church and someone who is becoming a member of your church. An attender is a spectator. A member is a participant. An attender is a consumer, but a member is a contributor. . . . **You become a Christian by committing your life to Jesus Christ.** You become a church member by committing yourself to another group of Christians. Now it is not just a commitment to God; it is a commitment to other Christians. If you are going to become part of the church, you become part of a family. A family where you love . . . and where you are loved. . . . And all members, the Scripture says, belong to one another. It's called fellowship. The Greek word is the word *koinonia*. . . . It means being committed to each other just as we are committed to Jesus Christ. That is genuine fellowship. **Now there are three parts to the Christian life** . . . Believing (Acts 16:31), Belonging (Ephesians 2:19) . . . and then Becoming (Romans 8:29). . . . And a **Believer**

without a church family is an orphan. There should be no orphan Christians. You need to be part of a church family. . . . There are at least 30 commands in the New Testament that you cannot obey unless you are committed to a local body of believers. . . . You can't do that unless you have other believers around you. So in your church, you need to communicate the value of membership. And you do it by telling people the benefits of membership.

RESPONSE:

So, let me get this straight. Pastor Hudnall is suggesting that if you are a Christian and not a member of local church, you are an orphan. Well, just to be sure, I did a search on blueletterbible.org for every occurrence of the word "orphan" in the Authorized King James Bible. To my great surprise, the word did not even come up on the search. So I checked the New American Standard and other translations. The word came up, but in cross-referencing it to the Scriptures, the word orphan was translated as "fatherless." I also checked it against the Greek and once again it is the word "fatherless." So, you might ask, what's the difference?

Well let's go back and plug in the more accurate rendering of the word into Pastor Todd Hudnall's axiom. It would now have to read: **"A believer without a church family is fatherless."** Now, we are not referring to literal orphans which are fatherless. Rather this teaching by Warren's ambassador is referring to the spiritual definition of "orphan," or a believer in Christ who is supposedly an orphan. Is this true? Well, let's examine the relevant scriptures to find out.

> But **as many as received him, to them gave he power to become the sons of God**, even to them that believe on his name.[171]

---

171 John 1:12

For ye have not received the spirit of bondage again to fear; but **ye have received the Spirit of adoption,** whereby we cry, Abba, Father.[172]

And will be a Father unto you, and ye shall be my sons and daughters, saith the Lord Almighty.[173]

To redeem them that were under the law, that we might **receive the adoption of sons. And because ye are sons, God hath sent forth the Spirit of his Son into your hearts, crying, Abba, Father.**[174]

Having predestinated us unto the adoption of children by Jesus Christ to himself, according to the good pleasure of his will.[175]

Even if we were to use Todd Hudnall's definition of a Christian "orphan," he would not be referring to literal orphans; his intent is obviously spiritual orphans. Yet it is the height of hypocrisy to label believers without a local church as "orphans," when in fact it is Warren's purpose-driven church model that has created a host of "orphans" by purpose-driving them out of church after church, as evidenced in part by this documentation of how Rick Warren uses spiritual eugenics for his policy of selective reduction of saints he calls "resisters" and "pillars," along with his partner Dan Sutherland, who calls them "Sanballats." Valley View Christian Church, a PDC in Dallas, Texas, promotes "Creative Destruction," and the Assemblies of God call it, "We

---

172   Romans 8:15

173   2 Corinthians 6:18

174   Galatians 4:5–6

175   Ephesians 1:5

Build People" and "Transformation." For proof see: "Spiritual Euthanasia."[176]

Therefore, I think we would all be wise to let Jesus Christ and his apostle Paul define who is an orphan (fatherless) in a spiritual sense. And Jesus did come when He sent the Holy Spirit at Pentecost. So from that time forth *every* Christian ceases to be an orphan the nanosecond, or twinkling of an eye, they become a believer and remain so. Hudnall would have us believe that there are now two classes of Christians—one group that are members of a local church and therefore not fatherless vs. a group which remain orphans until they become a member of a local church. But the Bible teaches that without Christ, all men are orphans; in Christ, none are orphans. So there are two groups all right. All men who are Christ-less are orphans, and all men who are saved are now no longer orphans but adopted sons!!! And just like the Judaizers that both Jesus and Paul warned us about, and Paul even cursed, no sooner are Christians set free in Christ, than Rick Warren comes along and puts them right back into the bondage of the law, traditions, and philosophies of men—a program that would be a Pharisee's dream, shipwrecking the faith of many, putting them in a worse state, and disqualifying themselves for the ministry.

In conclusion, it is true that we are commanded to not forsake the assembling of ourselves another. But forsaking the assembling, or simply being in transit between churches, or being forced or purpose-driven out of a church does not make a Christian an orphan.

PASTOR BOB DEWAAYS COMMENTS:

The PDC redefines the church, and joining such a church that is more of a community gathering of religious consumers than a

---

176 www.letusreason.org/Current61.htm—This article is also posted on a number of ministries around the world. Just type the title in Google for a list of them.

gathering of the blood-bought children of God is not what the biblical passages have in mind. Since God wants us to gather together for true fellowship, and since according to 1 John 1 we only have that through the blood atonement, and since the PDC doesn't preach the blood atonement publicly, I would urge all people in PDC churches to leave those and find churches where the unsullied preaching of God's Word is found.

TODD HUDNALL:

Now most churches bring in new members accidentally. But if you are going to be a Purpose Driven church you do it intentionally. . . . There is a plan. . . . There is a process. . . . Develop a plan to assimilate new members. Assimilate is turning outsiders into insiders.

Proverbs 20:18 says, "Make plans by seeking advice."

There are 12 questions you need to ask about a membership class.

A strong membership class will grow a strong church. This is not a doctrine. Your goal is to impart a vision in people so that they will give you a commitment. Understand this is not a doctrinal class. It isn't about doctrine, it is about philosophy. . . . In my church, my wife actually teaches the class. . . . New members need to see your vision and your personal vision as the pastor. This is not a new believer's class. That class needs to explain what is a church. What are the purposes of the church. What are the benefits of being a member. They need to know the benefits. What are the requirements? What is the strategy? . . . Develop a membership covenant. Second Corinthians 6:5 says this: "they first gave themselves to the Lord, then by God's will they gave themselves to us." Now in a marriage ceremony, what is the most important part of the ceremony? The vows. The membership covenant are the vows of becoming a member.

RESPONSE:

So apart from the fact that Warren's membership covenant strays from scriptural commands regarding oaths, as we have outlined above, Warren is not even correct in his analogy of church membership to marriage.

First of all, a person becomes of member of the body of Christ the minute they become a Christian. There is no second membership. Yes we do identify with a local expression of the body and should not forsake the assembling of one another and should be accountable to a local church. But Warren has created a false analogy. In our spiritual marriage, Christ is the groom and the church is the bride. And each individual member of the body of Christ comprises the bride. So we, in effect, are married to Christ (technically we are betrothed until the marriage supper of the Lamb), *not to the church*. In Pastor Hudnall's example we would be married to ourselves.

If he wants to draw a comparison of church membership to marriage, then he would have to apply God hating divorce to his model, in which case members (whom he calls "resisters") cannot be removed from the church accept for unfaithfulness and immorality. Yet that is precisely what he advocates through his leadership training documents. A recent example is 165 members being recently ousted from Gardendale Baptist Church in Corpus Christi, Texas, because they opposed the teachings of Rick Warren.

Rick Warren raises the stakes by comparing church membership to marriage—the gravity of this false analogy is that all believers are *already* the bride of Christ, and Christ alone is the groom; the church is not the groom. This is heresy of the highest order. Here is what Richard Bennett, director of Berean Beacon and a former Roman Catholic priest, has to say about comparing marriage vows to church membership vows—the same mistake Roman Catholicism has made in usurping the role and the authority of the church from Christ Himself:

Control in Conscience on the same level as Vows to God
Warren's Purpose Driven Megachurch program is "religion" in its worse possible understanding of the term. Like unto the Church of Rome it is a religion of control over the souls of men and women. The Roman Church gets people in by her sacraments and once in, she exercises her control by her Canon Law. The method of Warren is to win multitudes with a sham gospel (which we will document below), and then to control them with "a membership covenant." **The membership covenant is explained "in the same way" as marriage vows. Warren's teaching is,**

"The most important part of a marriage ceremony is when the man and woman exchange vows. Before witnesses and God, they make certain promises to each other. This covenant between them is the essence of the marriage. In the same way, I believe the essence of church membership is contained in the willingness to commit to a membership covenant. It is the most important element of our membership class."[177]

To put commitment to a church on the same level as marriage vows is utterly immoral. Marriage vows are a creation ordinance from God, in the Scripture there are no vows instituted by God regarding obedience to the pastor(s) of a church. Though the Pharisees imposed burdens on the people, they never came anywhere near demanding a submission on the same level as the vows of marriage. To demand obedience at a level God reserves to Himself in His creation ordinance of marriage is immoral. However until these false vows of membership are exposed for what they are, these vows, through false guilt will augment the increase in numbers of this new

---

177   www.pastors.com/article.asp?ArtID=3181

type of a Megachurch founded and implemented by Warren. . . . The false genius of Warren is to pretend to stand in God's place so as to control the souls of men and women. People are led to believe that their vow to church faithfulness is a vow to God just like a marriage vow. This is the ultimate tool of those who desire to have dominion of multitudes. Entice people into a system and then with persuasive techniques show them the necessity of committing themselves to loyalty to the system by means of a vow. Men and women think because they have made such a vow or covenant, if they criticize the church that they will have sinned against God. The church system thus uses these false vows for control of conscience of the members. Such so called church vows or covenants are false and void. Since in Revelation 17 we learn that Romanism will gather into herself the whole of apostate Christendom, called "Mystery Babylon," we suspect that what we are seeing is not just a movement, but that it is indeed the beginning of an apostate empire that can easily work with the Church of Rome and be one of her daughters.[178]

Bob DeWaay, pastor of Twin Cities Fellowship and author of *Redefining Christianity: Understanding the Purpose Driven Movement,* does an excellent treatment on oaths in his new book in the chapter entitled "Redefining Christian Commitment," further refuting Hudnall and Warren's teachings regarding oaths and vows as they apply to the individual Christian.

TODD HUDNALL:

Now at Saddleback there are four requirements for membership:

---

178   Richard Bennet, *Adulation of Man* e-mail to James Sundquist, November 24, 2004

First of all, that you have a personal relationship with Jesus Christ as your Lord and Savior.

Second of all you must be baptized in water as a public symbol of your faith.

Third of all you must complete the membership Class 101.

Fourth, you must SIGN the commitment to abide by the membership covenant. . . .

Now would you rather have the complainers leave or the committed followers leave? I would rather have the complainers leave and the followers stay! And that is what a membership class does. Now, when you establish and adopt a membership class, you are deciding who's gonna stay. It is about philosophy and strategy. Because people and churches rarely divide over doctrine; they usually divide over philosophy and strategy. So here is the Saddleback covenant. You should have this in your manual. . . . **Relationships are the glue that keep people in the church. . . . So, we need to close the back door of our church by getting people into small groups. . . . Don't apologize for asking people to make a commitment. You make the class so good that they will want to come to the class.**

RESPONSE:

Complainers vs. followers. This is also addressed above in an earlier paragraph. Let me just add that many of these "complainers" had legitimate biblical grievances. So yes, I would much rather have these people in the church who are not afraid to sound the alarm when they detect false teachings. In response to a question from the congregation about what to do with people who are already members, Hudnall says that they don't have to take the membership class. Yet saints all over the U.S., and Canada, in fact, are being removed or marginalized because they won't sign Warren's new covenants. Also see Paul Proctor's article on relationships: "Religious Relativism."

Finally at the end of the sessions, Todd Hudnall tells us that great leaders in Rick Warren's purpose-driven church model must rightly divide or handle the truth. He quotes Paul's instructions to Timothy, which states: Study to shew thyself approved unto God, a workman that needeth not to be ashamed, rightly dividing the word of truth."[179]

But I find this admonition almost beyond belief. This document proves that both Warren and Hudnall have distinctly *not* rightly divided or handled the truth. So these workers do need to be workmen ashamed and should be disqualified and silenced according Paul's teachings in Scripture.

Hudnall continues to ram home the same mantra we have heard all over the world that the vision of the pastor determines who stays and who leaves the church. But once again, this is a blatant usurping of power and abuse of spiritual authority. The Holy Spirit holds the authority of who goes and who stays in a church. Church discipline, according to Scripture, does give instructions on grounds for being expelled from a church — but this must be on moral grounds with documentation and two or more witnesses. And even then, a path of restoration is created should the disciplined person repent and/or make restitution. A difference in philosophy of ministry can NEVER be the grounds for biblically driving a person from the church.

We receive a flood of e-mails from pastors and Christians admonishing us for not having exercised Matthew 18 before publishing these findings (see Appendix E). I continue to be shocked how many shepherds of God's sheep do not know that Matthew 18

---

179   2 Timothy 2:15

pertains primarily to a private matter or sin between two brothers, not a public matter of teachings that are no longer private, but are rather very public. Scripture dictates public false teaching requires public exposure and warning. And even Matthew 18 would become public if the offending brother remains unrepentant. So, for those people who are still not convinced, I and many others already did directly confront Rick Warren, Todd Hudnall, John Jackson, and Phil Walker—twice. None have repented, none have responded, except finally Todd Hudnall, who did read this commentary but still maintains his defense of Rick Warren and his purpose-driven church and himself. He also refused to address any of my documentation. And though his letter was courteous, in contrast to most letters I receive from pastors (which are vile), he nevertheless accused me of attacking a brother. (I address the typical letter I receive from pastors accusing me of attacking a brother in Appendix D.) None have made restitution. So grounds are already established to make this public, whichever biblical passage you wish to invoke regarding church discipline.

Chapter 10

Alliances

Thomas Trask

General Superintendent of Assemblies of God

Tom Trask, general superintendent of the Assemblies of God Church and overseer of Assemblies of God which credentialed Pastor Todd Hudnall, helped spearhead the Centennial of the Azusa Street Revival in April 2006 in Los Angeles, where Rick Warren will be a keynote speaker. Some of the other apostate teachers invited to speak at this conference include Kenneth Copeland, T. D. Jakes, Bill Hamon (Apostolic and Prophetic Ministry Today,[180] Roman Catholic Francis MacNutt,[181] Jack Hayford, David Cho, Crello Dollar. See www.azuzsastreet100.net/events.htm for speaker roster.

Here Are More Examples of Rick Warren's Partnerships

♦ **August Turak** (New Ager) — Warren voted $100,000 Grand prize (unanimously) Templeton Foundation *Power of Purpose* Awards, 2004
♦ **Peter Drucker**
♦ **Philip Yancey**[182]

---

180   See www.deceptioninthechurch.com/newapostolic.html#bhamon for exposé on his teachings.

181   See "The Powers Behind Alpha, Vineyard, and the 'TE'" — www.users.globalnet.co.uk/~emcd/index31.htm

182   www.takeheed.net/YANCEY%20&%20lasciviousness.htm

- **Richard Foster**[183]
- **Rwanda:** first purpose-driven nation — President Paul Kagame, Summer 2005[184]
- **Bill Hybels** who promotes occultist Carl Jung (MBTI) and gave Muslim cleric a platform; spoke with Rick Warren and Blanchard at Willowcreek Sumulcast Summit, August 2005
- **Richard Abanes** — *Rick Warren and the Purpose that Drives Him* which promotes Rick Warren and slanders critics. Rick Warren promotes this book. James Walker, president of Watchman Fellowship, endorses Richard Abanes' book on Rick Warren.
- **Youth Specialities**[185]
- **Nicky Gumbel** — ALPHA COURSE[186]
- **Ken Blanchard**[187] — the featured speaker at First Assembly of God Church in Phoenix on November 27, 2005. I listened to this sermon on compact disc. I was so shocked and dismayed at the list of false teachers he embraced in this speech, I was compelled to write Tommy Barnett, their senior pastor, who had invited him. To date he has not responded to any of my e-mails or follow-up inquiries. Here are some excerpts from that letter:

December 9, 2005

Dear Pastor Tommy Barnett,

I just finished hearing the CD of Ken Blanchard speaking at your church recently.

I can only hope you are simply not aware of Ken Blanchard's

---

183 www.abrahamic-faith.com/James/Richard-Foster.html

184 www.time.com/time/archive/preview/0,10987,1093746,00.html

185 www.lighthousetrailsresearch.com/pdym.htm for comprehensive list of Ken Blanchard's New Age endorsements

186 For complete expose see www.users.globalnet.co.uk/~emcd/index5.htm

187 www.crossroad.to/Quotes/management/blanchard.htm

teachings and endorsements, including many he touted in his sermon to your congregation.

The most startling of all was his glowing view of Nelson Mandela. Are you aware that Mandela is a devout Marxist? Here is a quote from Mandela . . . can you possibly think as Christian that Blanchard would be his devotee?

"When you don't feel good about yourself, it is hard to feel good about anything or anyone else. . . . The only way to get out of this vicious cycle is to begin to believe in ourselves. . . . You are a child of God. . . . We are all meant to shine as children do. We are born to manifest the glory of God that is within us. It's not just in some of us it's in everyone. . . .

"Don't wait therefore for someone to tell you how wonderful you are. Just simply believe it, know it! Look deep within yourself. As we get to know and affirm ourselves for who we are, we become aware of the divinity that we share. What better place to find God than within ourselves."[188]

I find it equally astonishing that you or at least one wise among your congregation would not stand up and challenge Ken Blanchard's glowing endorsement of Norman Vincent Peale, a mentor to Robert Schuller, whose heresies are well-known. Blanchard further endorses, in his sermon to your congregation, Rick Warren (SHAPE), Bill Hybels, and Zig Ziglar, all three of whom promote occultist Carl Jung's Temperament Divination and Personality Profiling. I proved that Warren is a false teacher in my last e-mail to you. Blanchard also promotes Jung via DISC Profiling, invented by Wonder Woman comic strip author William Moulton Marsden, who used Jung archetypes to create a female heroine who put men in bondage.[189]

---

188   www.takeheed.net/news17.htm

189   www.crossroad.to/articles2/05/text/peace-un-2.htm

Blanchard also spoke glowingly of John Ortberg, who signed a letter[190] to President Bush appealing to him to give some of the land of Israel to the Palestinians, bringing a curse upon himself from God to anyone who tampers with Israel's God-given boundaries. (God has married ["Beulah"] that land to Israel . . . no one else has a right to divide it up . . . read Psalm 83 if you doubt what God will do to those who dare to carve up the land of Israel.) Blanchard also commends Bob Buford, whose account and defense of Mother Teresa (95%) [percentage represents Buford's idea that she only need 5% to close the gap to 100% between her and the Lord], who saw no reason to convert a Buddhist, is beyond the pale.

I remain shocked and saddened that you would not know about at least some of these false teachers that Blanchard promotes and endorses. I was compelled to bring this all to the attention of the listeners of Sonlife Radio Network (72 stations), and will continue to do so in the upcoming national radio interviews I will be doing in 2006 exposing Rick Warren's global PEACE plan vs. Scripture.

I hope and pray that you take heed to my words and those of Dr. Opal Reddin in her October 27, 2005, open letter of appeal and warning to all Assembly of God churches, which she wrote on her deathbed, one month before she was promoted to Glory. [Dr. Reddin was a matriarch in the Assemblies of God denomination]. I have spent thousands of hours researching these men's teachings. I also hope that you go before your own congregation and repent for having brought Ken Blanchard to

---

190 Support for a Palestinian state within the present borders of Israel and at the expense of Israel is also a common view within the Church Growth movement, as evidenced by a July 23, 2002, letter to President Bush containing the following statement signed by John Ortberg: "We commend your stated support for a Palestinian state with 1967 borders, and encourage you to move boldly forward so that the legitimate aspirations of the Palestinian people for their own state may be realized."
Source: www.northpark.edu/centers/middle/mideast.letter_to_bush.htm

speak to and mingle with your flock.

> Kindest regards in Christ,
> James Sundquist
> Director, Rock Salt Publishing

- ◆ **Faith Based Initiative** — which will dock neatly with Rick Warren's SHAPE program and his databasing his members
- ◆ **President Bush** — who has said Islam is a religion of peace and thinks surrendering the land God gave to Israel will bring peace.
- ◆ **Chuck Colson** — ECT signatory
- ◆ **Hugh Ross** — astronomer. For documentary exposé on Dr. Hugh Ross' false teachings see, James Sundquist's "Does God Expect Man to be Able to Tell Time? The Age of the Earth and the Future of the Earth"[191]
- ◆ **Roman Catholic Church** — Here is a quote from Rick Warren, who addressed 2,400 theologically conservative Anglicans on November 12, 2005, at the *Hope and a Future* conference of the Anglican Communion Network, at the David L. Lawrence Convention Center, during an interview:

> I really do feel that these people are brothers and sisters in God's family. I am looking to build bridges with the Orthodox Church, looking to build bridges with the Catholic Church, with the Anglican church, and say "What can we do together that we have been unable to do by ourselves?' "[192]

For extensive documentation on Roman Catholicism and Rick Warren's alliance, see Richard Bennett's *Berean Beacon* website[193]

---

191   www.nwcreation.net/articles/theageofearth.html

192   www.post-gazette.com/pg/05316/605324.stm

193   www.bereanbeacon.org/articles/rick_warren_purpose_driven.htm

and Roger Oakland's Understand the Times site, particularly *Upon This Rock: Biblical Christianity and Catholicism* (7 DVDs/12 presentations).[194] I also refer you to Factnet for more information on Roman Catholicism.[195]

Nonbelievers Too Can Be Saved, Says Pope

"Whoever seeks peace and the good of the community with a pure conscience, and keeps alive the desire for the transcendent, will be saved even if he lacks biblical faith, says Benedict XVI."[196]

This is a supremely ironic and hypocritical statement, given that when this pope was Cardinal Ratzinger, as guardian of doctrine for Roman Catholicism, he issued the following instructions: "The Vatican told Roman Catholic theologians that it will not tolerate public dissent from church teachings."[197] It should not come as a surprise to pastors promoting Rick Warren's programs that dissent is not tolerated in purpose-driven churches either, as I point out in my "Spiritual Euthansia" article.

The irony of Pope Benedict's statement is further compounded by the fact that the Council of Trent, which is still binding, anathematizes everyone who is not Roman Catholic, wherein no one can be saved unless they are Roman Catholic. This contradiction could not be more clear. Why then is Rick Warren going to build a bridge to this religion to advance his global PEACE plan?

---

194 http://understandthetimes.org/Merchant2/merchant.mvc?Screen=PROD&Store_Code=UTTS&Product_Code=UTRDVD&Category_Code=DVD

195 http://www.factnet.org/discus/messages/3/8816.html?11144486160

196 November 30, 2005, www.zenit.org/english/visualizza.phtml?sid=80888; special thanks to Be Alert newsletter

197 Dave Hunt, *Global Peace and the Rise of the Antichrist* (Harvest House, 1990), p. 138.

- **Bono** — rock star who leads the multitudes in singing his lyrics: "Jesus, Jew, Mohammed — all true. Jesus, Jew, Mohammed — all true . . ."[198]
- **Christian & Missionary Alliance**
- **National Association of Evangelicals aka NAE** — Ted Haggard, president, 45,000 churches, 30 million members[199]
- **General Baptist Convention**
- **Evangelical Covenant**
- **Assemblies of God denomination**
- **Southwest Baptist Theological Seminary**
- **Baptist World Alliance**
- **Boyd Pelley** — Life Together Online[200] and family pastor of The Church on Rush Creek in Arlington, Texas.
- **Emerging Church**[201]

[Note: This is by far only a partial listing of the alliances Rick Warren has formed.]

There are a host of Scriptures which warn us against unholy alliances . . . both in the Old and New Testaments. Here are two:

> Be ye not unequally yoked together with unbelievers: for what fellowship hath righteousness with unrighteousness? and what communion hath light with darkness? And what concord hath Christ with Belial? or what part hath he that believeth with an infidel? And what agreement hath the temple of God with idols? for ye are the temple of the living God; as God hath said,

198 Paul Proctor, "Taking Your Kids Out of Public Schools Is Not Enough!" — www.worldviewweekend.com/secure/cwnetwork/article.php?ArticleID=399

199 "Dominionism and the Rise of Christian Imperialism" — www.discernment-ministries.org/ChristianImperialism.htm

200 www.churchteams.com
www.zoomerang.com/recipient/survey.zgi?p=A233G3K14JNM

201 www.crossroad.to/articles2/05/peace-un-2.htm

I will dwell in them, and walk in them; and I will be their God, and they shall be my people. Wherefore come out from among them, and be ye separate, saith the Lord, and touch not the unclean thing; and I will receive you.[202]

And he charged them, saying, Take heed, beware of the leaven of the Pharisees, and of the **leaven of Herod. [Religious-political alliances and merging church and state vs. separation of church and state].**[203]

If Rick Warren's PEACE plan came directly from God, then why is Warren obtaining part of it from man, especially unredeemed man? This would be tantamount to Moses going to the Israelites for the rest of the blueprints for the Ark of the Covenant or the tabernacle, or Solomon getting the blueprints for the temple from the Philistines, or Ezekiel obtaining the blueprints for the millennial temple from the nations surrounding Israel.

Why is Rick Warren seeking counsel from the ungodly when Scripture warns the believer not to: **"Blessed is the man that walketh not in the counsel of the ungodly,** nor standeth in the way of sinners, nor sitteth in the seat of the scornful."[204]

Why is Rick Warren supporting a $100,000 Grand Prize to August Turak (a known and published New Ager), and rewarding Ken Blanchard (an endorser of a number of New Age books and a promoter of the occult-based DISC Profiler[205]) with authority to help train his billion-man Christian army? Scripture warns us: "Whoso **rewardeth** evil for good, evil shall not depart from his house."[206]

---

202   2 Corinthians 6:14–17

203   Mark 8:15

204   Psalm 1.1

205   www.crossroad.to/articles2/05/peace-un-2.htm

206   Proverbs 17:13

Chapter 11

Hope

Just when it appears that there is no hope because of Rick Warren's takeover of churches throughout the world as he launches his global PEACE plan, I received the following letter from a pastor's wife in Dallas, Texas, whose family left Valley View Christian Church in Dallas, Texas, a congregation that her husband had served for nearly thirty-four years, along with a couple hundred others. Consequently, they have since formed a new church.

Now I must emphasize that many who left this church did not do so with the knowledge that it was *the influence* of Rick Warren's teachings and programs which were behind the changes at the church — until after they left, as much of the infiltration of Warren's ideas (including the transformation process) did not *appear* to be dangerous at first.

This letter should not only encourage the saints throughout the country who have been wounded by this movement, but also help equip them to be brave enough to take similar action. The following account is eerily similar to the accounts both Kaycia Key and I have heard reported and documented from Christians who have left or were purpose-driven out of other purpose-driven churches around the country:

December 14, 2005 and January 9, 2006

Hi James,

Our newly founded church, Cornerstone, is doing very well, has such a sweet spirit. We have over 250 members and we are meeting in facilities provided by Dallas Christian College. We have to use the gymnasium for worship services because it's the largest area to meet. We're too big for their chapel. We also have refugees from a myriad of other churches.

Ron and I are having an Open House this weekend to try to thank everyone for all the love and support we've received . . . so that has kept me pretty busy.

I finally got to get a little further into your book and another one that someone else sent which echoes the same concerns you have. I am so grateful to you for identifying some of the causes of my fear and concern for the Lord's church. The Deceiver certainly has come as an "angel of light" in these days.

I recently read an article in *Christianity Today,* five pages of Rick Warren's Global Plan to end world poverty. It was sad and frightening to read all those pages and only one mention of Jesus . . . a mention about how Rick Warren was there to restore the hands and feet to the body. And as you point out, his theology is definitely skewed. Have seen numerous articles corroborating your book. . . .

Many who left Valley View Christian Church did so in great part because the leadership had developed an irrational and irrecoverable rupture in our common faith, belief and vision of Christ's church **after** we studied and implemented the *Purpose Drive Life* by Rick Warren.

The church had been experiencing problems between the elders and the congregation and people were quietly (and some not so quietly) beginning to leave. When the elders brought in a new preaching minister people grew more unhappy and then after we did the purpose-driven programs the rift developed into the rupture of faith and our vision for Christ's church to the point a "re-visioning" even the foundational charter. To try to overcome this growing rift the elders, and Ron and I, agreed to submit ourselves to a biblically-based reconciliation process under the direction of a professional Christian reconciliation group to try to overcome this mindset which had come upon the church. But three days later the elders reversed their decision and asked Ron to resign, with six months severance or be fired and receive two months severance. Ron, my husband and senior minister, said that under these circumstances, they would have to fire him, because he said he could not resign when he had lived up to his end of the agreement. Ron Key did not, as some may thought (or been erroneously told) start a new church, but was asked to become the minister of the new church, once it was founded.

Since then the church has grown to about 275–300, several of whom were refugees from other churches in the area who were also leaving because of many of the same issues with leadership that had developed in their respective congregations after purpose-driven programs. We are also now being able to share in love with more people about the perils of Warren's programs. Believers, who sensed something amiss, but were not aware of the dangers in his teachings and who knew nothing (like me) of the congregations that have developed splits after having implemented his "purpose-driven" ideas. As one of our members and past elder at VVCC stated, "The question is not whether the congregation will obey their elders, but whether the elders will obey Christ."

—Kaycia Key [reprinted by permission]

The ultimate question is not whether Warren's global PEACE plan or the *Purpose Driven Life* bears witness with spirit of the elders or members of a church, but whether Rick Warren's teachings bear witness to the scriptural teachings of Jesus.

Chapter 12

Conclusion

Rick Warren, through his *Purpose Driven Life, Purpose Driven Church,* and his global PEACE plan, has usurped the mantle and authority belonging only to Christ, not unlike the papacy, which has presumptuously set up the pope as the vicarious head of the church. We appeal to all Christians to sound the alarm on His holy hill! God is a jealous God, and Christ—not Rick Warren—will secure the ultimate victory and will establish his own kingdom, so help us God!

> But I fear, lest by any means, as the serpent beguiled Eve through his subtilty, so your minds should be corrupted from the simplicity that is in Christ. . . . And no marvel; for Satan himself is transformed into an angel of light. Therefore it is no great thing if his ministers also be transformed as the ministers of righteousness; whose end shall be according to their works.[207]

> Let no man beguile you of your reward in a voluntary humility and worshipping of angels, intruding into those things which he hath not seen, vainly puffed up by his fleshly mind.[208]

---

207 2 Corinthians 11:3,14–15

208 Colossians 2:18

For the time will come when they will not endure sound doctrine; but after their own lusts shall they heap to themselves teachers, having itching ears.[209]

Additional Valuable Resources Which Address Rick Warren's Global PEACE Plan

Southwest Radio Ministries
www.swrc.com

Search for "Rick Warren" in the radio broadcasts and documents and their Purpose-Driven Church/Life Resource Center. Also look for their new tract, "Is Your Church Going Purpose Driven? How Can You Tell?" See also Warren Smith interview on Southwest Radio Ministries, December 15–16, 2005.[210]

Pastor Bob DeWaay
Critical Issues Commentary
www.twincityfellowship.com/index.php

Twin City Fellowship has just launched a "discernment tool" so people can check Rick Warren's *Purpose Driven Life* against Scripture. This is a new discernment resource that will help you navigate *The Purpose Driven Life* on your own, page by page, day by day—all 40 Days of Purpose. This tool allows you to be the Berean you want to be without wasting precious hours hunting for the texts. What you find when you read and compare may surprise you.[211] See also, "The Dangers of Spiritual Formation and Spiritual Disciplines," Issue 91, November/December 2005 by Bob DeWaay.[212]

---

209 2 Timothy 4:3

210 www.swrc.com/broadcasts/2005/december.htm

211 www.cicministry.org/berean/php

212 www.cicministry.org/commentary/issue91.htm

Pastor Gary Gilley
"Gospel According to Warren" — July 2005 Newsletter[213]

Berit Kjos
Warren's PEACE plan and UN Goals — Part 3 of 4
"Whom do we serve?"[214]

See also "Your Comments" section; scroll down to "From Jane."
She writes: "When I read Rick Warren's peace plan, I must say I
was deeply alarmed, especially because his worldwide influence
deceives so many unsuspecting people."[215]

Lighthouse Trails Ministry
"Rick Warren's global PEACE plan"[216]

Ray Yungen
"A Time of Departing, Expanded Second Edition"[217]
[includes chapter on Rick Warren], March 2006

Lynn & Sarah Leslie
"What Is Transformation"[218]

Way of Life Ministry
"Rick Warren's Global Vision,
Purple Haze, and New Age Association"[219]

213   www.svchapel.org/Resources/Articles/read_articles.asp?ID=112

214   www.crossroad.to/articles2/05/peace-un-3.htm

215   www.crossroad.to/text/responses/archive/purpose-1.htm

216   www.lighthousetrailsresearch.com/peaceplan.htm

217   www.lighthousetrailsresearch.com/atimeofdeparting.htm

218   www.newswithviews.com/Leslie/sarah.htm

219   www.wayoflife.org/fbns/rickwarren-globalvision.html

James Sundquist interview by *Prophezine* magazine[220]

Crosstalk, VCY America[221]

Loren Davis[222]

Moriel Ministries
"Rick Warren Connections—Especially to the Ecumenical Third Wave New Apostolic Reformation (NAR) and 'Positive Thinking' Movement"[223]

Dean Gotcher
"Diaprax: the dialectic process and *praxis*"[224]
"Defeating the Diaprax"[225]

Mike Oppenheimer
"A global PEACE plan"[226]

Robert Klenck, M.D.
"What's Wrong with the 21st Century Church?"[227]
Rick Warren's Purpose Driven Life: A Rebuttal[228]

---

220 www.abrahamic-faith.com/James/James_prophezine_interview.html

221 www.vcyamerica.org/crosstalk/event_popup.cfm?programid=1130

222 www.lorendavis.com

223 www.moriel.org/articles/discernment/church_issues/rick_warren_connections.htm

224 www.authorityresearch.com

225 www.christianmedianetwork.com/gotcher.htm

226 www.letusreason.org/Popteac26.htm

227 www.crossroad.to/News/Church/Klenck1.html
     www.crossroad.to/News/Church/Klenck2.html

228 www.johnecoleman.org/Bob%20Klenck%20Page.htm

Roger Oakland
"Purpose Driven Ecumenism?"[229]

Richard Bennett (former Roman Catholic priest)
"The Adulation of Man in the the Purpose Driven Life"[230]
"Purpose Driven Life: Demeaning the Very Nature of God"[231]

Former Catholics for Christ[232]

Paul Proctor
July 9, 2005, interview on John Loeffler's "Steeling of the Mind" radio show.[233]

Mac Dominick
"Rebuilding the Tower of Babel"[234]

Discernment Ministries, Inc.
"The Necessity of Separation from Heresy"
Discernment Newsletter – January/February 2006[235]

The Conservative Theological Journal
"A Critique of the Purpose Driven Life" by James Sundquist
Part I – August 2005 / Part II – December 2005
Who's Driving the Purpose Driven Church book review
December 2005

---

229 www.understandthetimes.org/current_transcripts/text/sep2005/1785.shtml

230 http://www.bereanbeacon.org/articles_pdf/rick_warren_purpose_driven.pdf

231 www.bereanbeacon.org/articles_pdf/rick_warren_purpose_driven_2.pdf

232 www.geocities.com/Heartland/Plains/2594/

233 www.lighthousetrailsresearch.com/PaulProctorInterview.mp3

234 www.cuttingedge.org/news/rtb1.html
www.cuttingedge.org/news/rtb2.html
www.cuttingedge.org/news/rtb3.html

235 www.discernment-ministries.org/NLJanFeb_2006.htm

John Maxwell's Teachings

John Maxwell's teachings are at the core of much of Warren's global PEACE plan and purpose-driven programs and philosophy, and is touted by both Todd Hudnall (Assembly of God) and Dr. John Jackson (American Baptist). So I am devoting more extensive treatment to him in this documentary. John Maxwell is another major player in social engineering. Mr. Hudnall believes ministry starts with good leadership. Hudnall endorses John Maxwell a second time at the end of his PDC conference when he states: "Everything rises and falls with leadership." But what kind of leader in ministry touts well-known eugenicist Thorndike, as John Maxwell does in his *"good"* book?

Besides Edward Thorndike (evolutionist, eugenicist, humanist, atheist), the parade of false teachers and teachings that Maxwell promotes in his books is quite staggering. Just some of them include: Norman Vincent Peale (33rd Degree Mason), Robert Schuller, Richard Foster, Agnes Sanford (pantheist and Carl Jung disciple), Napolean Hill, New Age psychologist James Allen, Kay Arthur (THRIVE), Zig Ziglar, Bill Hybels, and, of course, Rick Warren. The Assembly of God (and of course all Christians) should be be particularly horrified by Agnes Sanford's definition of the baptism of the Holy Spirit (see Richard Howe's article below). If there is any doubt that John Maxwell is a false teacher, read the following documentaries:

♦ **Midwest Outreach** article entitled "Some Concerns About John C. Maxwell" by Richard G. Howe.[236]
♦ **Berit Kjos** article "Strange Journeys: Jane Fonda, John Maxwell, Norma McCorvey, and Scott Peck—what do they have in common?"[237]
♦ **Steve Muse**—Eastern Regional Watch—an article entitled "The Temptation to Love Another."[238]

Behavior Modification

On page 124 of his book *Developing the Leaders Around You*, John Maxwell endorses behaviorism psychologist Edward Thorndike. Maxwell states: "Behaviors immediately rewarded increase in frequency; behaviors immediately punished decrease in frequency." Here is more what Thorndike believed:

> **Edward L. Thorndike,** Cattell's famous protégé, also adopted Galton's views on inherited intelligence. As a true believer in race science and evolution, he believed that man was an animal that could be trained as an animal. Thus, he invented the stimulus-response technique of behavioral education. He wrote in 1911:
>
> "Nowhere more truly than in his mental capacities is man a part of nature. His instincts, that is, his inborn tendencies to feel and act in certain ways, show throughout marks of kinship with the lower animals, especially with our nearest relatives physically, the monkeys. His sense-powers show no new creation. His intellect we have seen to be a simple though extended variation from the general animal sort. This again is presaged by the similar variation in the case of the monkeys. Amongst

---

236   www.rapidnet.com/~jbeard/bdm/exposes/maxwell/general.htm

237   www.crossroad.to/articles2/05/journeys.htm#maxwell

238   www.erwm.com/Temptation_for_Another.htm

the minds of animals that of man leads, not as a demigod from another planet, but as a king from the same race."

Thus, the idea that man was made in God's image went out the school window. Both Cattell and Thorndike had fathers who were Christian ministers, so they knew the Bible very well. Their apostasy destroyed American education. Thus, with America's top educators adapting the ideas of eugenics to the problems of education, eugenics as scientific racism acquired widespread respectability. It should also be noted that the IQ test was a direct result of the eugenics enterprise, serving as a means of sifting out the mentally superior."[239]

Note that John Maxwell quotes Edward Thorndike. Edward Thorndike also said: "Schools would serve as 'instruments of managed evolution,' establishing conditions for selective breeding before the masses take things into their own hands."[240]

Thorndike was a eugenicist (selective breeding of humans which, of course, leads to population control, as in China), and ultimately he was racist at heart. Abortion is a modern, politically correct form of eugenics — the elimination of undesirables. Thorndike would oversee the training of more empirical characterologists than any other American. In a 1913 lecture, "Eugenics, with Special Reference to Intellect and Character," he sang the praises of the eugenics movement.[241]

As noted before, this is all repackaged in Dale Carnegie's *How to Win friends and Influence People,* whom Todd Hudnall also quotes and promotes. It is prosperity doctrine with more

239 See "Eugenics and the Christian Ethic" by Samuel L. Blumenfeld — www.sierratimes.com/cgi-bin/ikonboard/topic.cgi?forum=11&topic=5

240 Published essay by Edward Thorndike at Columbia University Teacher's College in 1911.

241 See "Good Genes Not Enough; Character Education needed for Race Betterment," — www.watch.pair.com/charter2.html

spin. I wonder how Maxwell and Hudnall would respond to the following:

Some saints who never became leaders "fulfilled" so God would be glorified:

1. The thief on the cross
2: "And others had trial of cruel mockings and scourgings, yea, moreover of bonds and imprisonment: They were stoned, they were sawn asunder, were tempted, were slain with the sword: they wandered about in sheepskins and goatskins; being destitute, afflicted, tormented; (Of whom the world was not worthy:) they wandered in deserts, and in mountains, and in dens and caves of the earth. And these all, having obtained a good report through faith, **received not the promise.**"[242] **Few if any of these became leaders. If anything, they went the other way and became slaves, prisoners, and persecuted.**
3. "Hearken, my beloved brethren, Hath not God chosen the poor of this world rich in faith, and heirs of the kingdom which he hath promised to them that love him. But ye have despised the poor. Do not rich men oppress you, and draw you before the judgment seats?"[243]
4. The saints in Revelation who loved their lives not unto death were far more commended many mighty men (few of which will enter the kingdom of God) — these saints in Smyrna and Philadelphia whom the Lord had nothing against — for the most part did not become leaders. Wouldn't I rather be the Christian God called me to be than become a leader if this is not what God has for me? So my question for Mr. Maxwell is, why would we want to become the type of person that God says very few of whom will enter the kingdom?

---

242   Hebrews 11:36–39

243   James 2:5–6

5. Not many should be teachers (leaders) as they will receive a stricter accounting. So if we are not called to be leaders, how will God be glorified—as though God is not already glorified with or without any pitiful efforts of man or his meager filthy rags works?

Lessons in Leadership from the Word of God—The Maxwell Leadership Bible—Notes and Articles by John Maxwell—New King James Version.

Here is the advertisement:

No matter who you are, someone is following you as you follow Jesus. *God is glorified when you fulfill your capacity for leadership!* Discover your astonishing potential to impact the world for Christ (emphasis mine).

Where, Mr. Maxwell, do you find in Scripture that God is glorified when we fulfill our capacity for leadership? What about the humble servants who were obedient to the Lord?

♦ The widow (and her mite).
♦ The woman (prostitute) who broke the alabaster jar and anointed Jesus' feet.
♦ The apostle Paul.

How would Mr. Maxwell respond to the following Scriptures?

For I through the law am dead to the law, that I might live unto God. I am crucified with Christ: nevertheless I live; yet not I, but Christ liveth in me: and the life which I now live in the flesh I live by the faith of the Son of God, who loved me, and gave himself for me. I do not frustrate the grace of God: for if righteousness come by the law, then Christ is dead in vain.[244]

---

244 Galatians 2:19–21

And they that are Christ's have crucified the flesh with the affections and lusts.[245]

But God forbid that I should glory, save in the cross of our Lord Jesus Christ, by whom the world is crucified unto me, and I unto the world.[246]

Not that I speak in respect of want: for I have learned, in whatsoever state I am, therewith to be content. I know both how to be abased, and I know how to abound: every where and in all things I am instructed both to be full and to be hungry, both to abound and to suffer need. I can do all things through Christ which strengtheneth me.[247]

So the apostle Paul says he has not yet achieved it, but John Maxwell tells us all that — even if we are not Christians — it is within our reach? Regarding Maxwell and Warren, why is it all of these people always have "principles" and "laws" of Christ? Don't they know it is not Christ's principles or laws that redeem us and ransom us out of darkness, but the *Person* **of Christ Himself** and the *Person* **of the Holy Spirit** that sanctifies who we are in Christ — not those who are outside of Christ.

Finally, it is not even surprising that Hudnall promotes John Maxwell, because the whole purpose-driven church and its clone, the Assemblies of God's Vision of Transformation and We Build People, practice their own version of Edward Thorndike's elimination of undesirables in the church. They simply rename the practice "blessed subtraction" or dealing with "resisters" and "pillars," or as Hudnall puts it "complainers."

---

245 Galatians 5:24

246 Galatians 6:14

247 Philippians 4:11–13

Rick Warren's Baseball Diamond

It is interesting that Warren picks an American sport. And though it is now popular in many countries, how does he explain his baseball diamond analogy to countries which either never heard of baseball as a sport or far prefer soccer?

Which team is on the Lord's side, the offense or the defense? How do you get to first base (CLASS 101)? Works of course—you have to hit a run. What if you hit a home run? Do you go immediately to home plate (CLASS 401)? And don't forget, you can also get to first base if the pitcher throws four balls—or hits you with the ball—so then you get to first base not on your works, but on another man's errors. Who is the umpire in this game analogy? What if he calls you out in three strikes and you never get to first base at all?

But let's say you somehow make it to first base. There you have to sign a covenant of membership in spite of Jesus' very strong warnings about oaths. But at any point in time you can be called out if you don't steal second base (CLASS 201), or batters that follow you are struck out or pop-flied out.

Let's say that you somehow make it to second base. Now you have to take another covenant pledging to tithe, in spite of the fact that Paul tells us to give *without* compulsion.

Then somehow—perhaps your own effort or that of a teammate's hit—you make it to third base. And what is third base? Still another covenant you must sign (CLASS 301). But this one is probably the worst, because you are forced to take a personality temperament profile, which is in effect practicing temperament divination. It is bad enough that you have to take the profile, but worse that Warren promotes it and makes it binding upon the membership of his church and an integral part of the training manual being presented to hundreds of thousands of churches all over the world.

Home plate is CLASS 401. But now they have CLASS 501. How do you get a fifth base into a four-base sport? And how many runs do you need to win? Whose side is the pitcher on? What if the batter is a good shortstop, but rarely if ever makes a hit? The game is rigged and tilted in favor of good batters. And does the other team get to bat?

Pastor John Jackson declared at this conference that "you get no credit for people [runners] left on base." Well this is troublesome for a least four reasons:

1. Why do you get credit at all, or even want the credit for someone getting saved (first base)?
2. Where in Scripture do we get permission to measure results which the PDC model insists on doing?
3. Jackson indicts his own model of using the analogy of a baseball diamond because the thief on the cross was stranded on first base without going to the other three bases, as were a host of martyrs and persecuted saints throughout the church age.
4. If you get no credit for leaving men stranded on base, that means you only get credit if they run all of the bases. So what he is really saying is you must take all three covenants (three bases), the worst being the third which requires you to practice magic arts.

While John Jackson has you virtually convinced that Warren's baseball diamond symbol is essential to the purpose-driven model which will work in any church, he tells us that his own church doesn't even use this baseball diamond. So much for confidence in your own product!! The bottom line is that Rick Warren's baseball diamond analogy raises more questions than it answers. It introduces more frightening requirements and consequences upon a Christian that are burdens far beyond what is written in Scripture, and it also introduces requirements which are distinctly *prohibited* in Scripture.

Hendrix and the Occult

Jimi Hendrix was deeply involved in occultism and mysticism. These themes permeated his music. His song "Voodoo Child" glorified voodoo practices such as out of body experiences.

> Well, I'm a voodoo child
> Lord, I'm a voodoo child
> The night I was born
> Lord, I swear the moon turned a fire red
> . . . My poor mother cried out now the gypsy was right
> And I seen her fall down right dead
> . . . 'Cause I'm a voodoo child
> Lord knows, I'm a voodoo child. . . .

In fact, Hendrix believed he was possessed by the devil. Girl-friend Fayne Pridgon said: **"He used to always talk about some devil or something was in him** . . . and having some root lady or somebody see if she could **drive this demon out of him."**[248]

Pharmaka (pharmakeia)

"The cause of death [of Jimi Hendrix] noted on the coroner's re-

---

248 Soundtrack from film Jimi Hendrix, interview with Fayne Pridgon, side 4, cited by Heartbeat of the Dragon, p. 50. Distributed by Way of Life Literature's Fundamental Baptist Information Service, 2001 — www.wayoflife.org/fbns/jimi-hendrix-experi-ence.html (emphasis mine)

port was inhalation of vomit after barbiturate intoxication."[249]

Scripture is very clear about *pharmaka*, the Greek term for "drugs." The *King James Version Study Bible* states the following about *pharmaka*:

> Witch (*mekashep*) denotes a form of magic. The root means "to cut up," and thus may refer to one who cuts up herbs and brews them for magical purposes (Gr., *Pharmaka*, drug). The term is used in Micah 5:12 for some such material as drugs or herbs used superstitiously to produce magical effects. The noun therefore means enchanter or sorcerer (Ex. 7:11; 22:18; 2 Chr. 33:6; Dan. 2:2; Mal. 3:5).

Also see:

> And the light of a candle shall shine no more at all in thee; and the voice of the bridegroom and of the bride shall be heard no more at all in thee: for thy merchants were the great men of the earth; **for by thy sorceries were all nations deceived.**[250]

Note: the word "sorceries" is rendered *pharmakeia* (original word: *farmakeiða*) in *Strong's Lexicon*:

1. the use or the administering of drugs
2. poisoning
3. sorcery, magical arts, often found in connection with idolatry and fostered by it
4. *metaph.* the deceptions and seductions of idolatry

---

249   www.classicbands.com/hendrix.html

250   Revelation 18:23

Spiritual Euthanasia Notes:

1. Pastor Dave Hawk—Brunswick Reformed Church, Brunswick, Ohio.[251] Incidents occurred with Susan Anderson April–June 2001. Testimony reconfirmed by e-mail from Susan Anderson March 11, 2005.
2. Confirmed by the testimony of Betty Erwin on Southwest Radio Ministries, March 1, 2005,[252] and letters dated November 7, 11, and 24, 2004, and January 6, 2005, by Betty Erwin to Mr. and Mrs. Brunson and another former pastor at Dallas First Baptist Church, and telephone interview March 2005.
3. Pastor Rev. Timothy S. Magnuson—Valley Baptist Church, Lakeland, Minnesota. Verified by letters from church and the families of Keith Thompson and Charles Thompson. Centered around October 22, 2002.
4. Pastor Micah Davison—Gardendale Baptist Church, Corpus Christi, Texas.[253] 165 members ousted on July 21, 2004.[254] Testimonies of ousted members Piedad Ymbert, B. J. Moore, Grady Jackson can be heard at Southwest Radio Ministries

---

251   www.b-r-c.org

252   www.swrc.com/broadcasts/2005/march.htm

253   www.reallifefellowship.org

254   www.sbcbaptistpress.org/bpnews.asp?ID=18997
      Corpus Christi Caller-Times, e-mail: neum@caller.com

website.[255] See also pages 193–194 of *Who's Driving the Purpose Driven Church?* by James Sundquist.[256]

5. Pastor Gary Clark—Eugene Christian Fellowship, Eugene, OR.[257] Confirmed in letters from and correspondence with Eugene Christian Fellowship leaders Tim Reich, executive pastor Jonathan Hatmaker, Discovery 301 Class (SHAPE) leader Mark Harpham, November 11–19, 2004

6. American Family Radio News, Tupelo, MS.[258] Radio news segment ran February 15, 2005.

7. Regarding Watchman on the Wall radio show—*Prophetic Observer*, February and March issues.[259]

8. Senior Pastor Randy Myers—New Hope Church, Bend, Oregon.[260] Correspondence with Pastors Josh Conn (February 3–23, 2005) and William Vermillion of The Evangelical Church, an NAE affiliate (February 26–March 12, 2005).

9. Pastor Mark Martin—Calvary Community Church, Phoenix, Arizona.[261] Testimony of Bear Frankson based on events since July 2004. Taped interview: February 18, 2005.

255 www.swrc.com/broadcasts/2003/september.htm

256 www.swrc.com
www.abrahamic-faith.com/False-Teachers.html

257 www.ecf.org

258 www.afr.net

259 Southwest Radio Ministries, P.O. Box 100, Bethany, OK 73008.
Telephone: 1-800-652-1144   e-mail: info@swrc.com

260 www.newhopeonline.net

261 www.netministries.org/see/churches.exe/ch19442
e-mail: calvary@calvaryphpx.com

Typical Attack from a Pastor Defending Purpose-Driven Model & Response

I have included this letter because it is one of the most common types of letters I receive from pastors who retaliate when I have tried to warn them of the dangers involved in the purpose-driven model. I believe my response as well as the responses from Chris Carmichael, Jacob Prasch, and Hadley Robinson can be very helpful in equipping saints who are in churches that are going purpose-driven and who receive similar challenges. This pastor has not responded since he was confronted.

Sent: Saturday, March 18, 2006 7:49 PM

Subject: RE: Rick Warren Global Peace Plan vs. Scripture FINAL PUBLISHED Documentary

James,
     After wrestling with Proverbs 26:4–5, I've opted to apply v. 5 by responding to your unsolicited spam:
     ◆ If your brother sins against you, go and show him his fault, just between the two of you. If he listens to you, you have won your brother over. — Matt 18:15

♦ Brothers, if someone is caught in a sin, you who are spiritual should restore him gently. But watch yourself, or you also may be tempted. —Galatians 6:1

♦ Now, dear brothers and sisters, I appeal to you by the authority of the Lord Jesus Christ to stop arguing among yourselves. Let there be real harmony so there won't be divisions in the church. I plead with you to be of one mind, united in thought and purpose. . . . For Christ didn't send me to baptize, but to preach the Good News—and not with clever speeches and high-sounding ideas, for fear that the cross of Christ would lose its power. —1 Corinthians 1:10–17

Spend more time preaching Jesus and less time gossiping (James 3) about guys who love Jesus and are on your own team (which may be a faulty assumption: 1 John 4:20).

———————————————

Pastor from a Church in California

Dear Pastor,

I believe it is biblically appropriate for me to respond to your e-mail. I have also sought a multitude of biblical counsel in which there is wisdom and have enclosed their responses as well.

I have a few of my own comments to your missive, but agree with Chris and Jacob's comments below.

1. In quoting Proverbs 26:4–5 intimating or implying that I am a "fool," I remind you of Jesus Christ's words: "But I say unto you, That whosoever is angry with his brother without a cause shall be in danger of the judgment: and whosoever shall say to his brother, Raca, shall be in danger of the council: **but whosoever shall say, Thou fool, shall be in danger of hell fire" (Matt. 5:22).**

2. Are you suggesting that I am bearing false witness

against a brother? God deems this an abomination. So you had better substantiate it, if you fear the Lord.

3. Your quote of 1 Corinthians 1:10–17 certainly does teach that we are to preserve unity in the Body of Christ, but never at the price of truth. Rick Warren is not telling the truth. Here are but a few examples:

I assure you that because I fear the Lord and he considers bearing false witness against a brother an abomination, that what I have written you better be true.

I would only ask that you be a good Berean (as we all must be and go directly to Scripture and read Warren's 40 Day examples he cites on pages 9–10 of his *Purpose Driven Life*, then read the actual biblical passages. I am not alone on this. A number of biblical scholars identified these errors of where Warren simply invented what those passages say. (I am sure you are familiar with the biblical passages of what God thinks about changing, adding or subtracting from God's Word — what He is "against').

I also invite you to simply read Jesus Christ's own warnings about taking oaths and signing covenants. (Many Christians throughout the U.S. and Canada have been removed from PDC churches because they decided to obey Jesus Christ).

"Again, ye have heard that it hath been said by them of old time, Thou shalt not forswear thyself, but shalt perform unto the Lord thine oaths: But I say unto you, Swear not at all; neither by heaven; for it is God's throne: Nor by the earth; for it is his footstool: neither by Jerusalem; for it is the city of the great King. Neither shalt thou swear by thy head, because thou canst not make one hair white or black. But let your communication be, Yea, yea; Nay, nay: **for whatsoever is more than these cometh of evil**" (Matt. 5:33–37).

And his apostle James reaffirms this same warning with dire consequences: "But above all things, my brethren, swear not, neither by heaven, neither by the earth, neither by any other oath: but let your yea be yea; and your nay, nay; **lest ye fall into condemnation**" (Jam. 5:12).

4. Regarding your comment that I sent this to you *unsolicited spam*—your e-mail address is posted on your denomination's website—i.e., it is already published and in the public forum. And as a pastor, are you telling me that you do not want to receive any e-mails that you don't agree with? Even if an inquiring brother was in error, instead of retaliating, why isn't it you "who are more spiritual" do as the apostle Paul or Stephen did and commended us to do, that is reason from Scripture where I am in error, so that I will be set free from the snare that we might *both* rejoice?

The main gripe with so-called spam is that it is "unsolicited." If Paul took this advice, precious few would have been saved or corrected if they were a brother, because who would ever ask to get rebuked? Nicodemus asked what he must do to be saved—one rare example of soliciting a response. Imagine Martin Luther waiting for permission to nail his unsolicited 95 theses on the Wittenburg door. If either Paul or Martin Luther had e-mail, I find in unthinkable that they would use it to send *only* e-mails when someone solicited him to send them a letter, as he certainly did not wait for permission to send all of the letters he did send by his own hand!

Finally, before I supply you with the other responses below, I am compelled to remind you of the following Scripture regarding Rick Warren:

"If there come any unto you, and bring not this doctrine, receive·him not into your house, neither bid him God speed: For he that biddeth him God speed is partaker of his evil deeds" (2 John 1:10–11).

One more thing, I did not personally attack you and did not even know where you stood regarding Rick Warren, I was simply sending you an ALERT that you might only need to heed if you were pursuing his teachings and programs.

Kindest regards in Christ,
James Sundquist
Director
Rock Salt Publishing

Dear Pastor:

Why is it so necessary for you to be extremely uncharitable towards Mr. Sundquist? I ask you, on what biblical basis do you try to twist a brother's words and redefine his ministry in order to construct your unfounded rebuke against him?

For starters, Mr. Sundquist has not "spammed" you, but has sent an urgent warning to fellow believers he loves in the Lord. For you to suggest otherwise, is to also imply that the apostle Paul sent an "unsolicited spam" to the Galatians to warn them against the Judaizers. You may disagree with Mr. Sundquist's biblical position on this matter, but to dismiss his correspondence as spam is without merit, and frankly shows your dishonesty in handling James' sincere concern for your denomination's spiritual well-being.

Secondly, you have horribly misused Scripture in your effort to dismiss James' position. Mr. Sundquist's correspondence to you is specifically dealing with false teaching being spread throughout the church, and not with a personal disagreement between two brothers (Matt. 18:15) or a confrontation over sin within a local body of believers (Gal. 6:1). Rather, the scripture that is more pertinent to James' approach is found in Romans 16:17: "*Mark them* which cause divisions and offenses *contrary to the doctrine which ye have learned;* and avoid them." This is just one of many scriptural directives on how

139

to deal with false teachers and their unbiblical doctrines (Titus 1:13; Eph. 5:11; Jude 3. etc.).

You see, Pastor, it is James' contention that Rick Warren is teaching contrary to biblical doctrine and that these teachings are causing division and confusion within the PDL churches, which James has carefully documented. Your outright dismissal of these facts because you don't like James' approach does not change the biblical foundation of James' arguments. More importantly, James is not alone in his criticism of Warren's teachings.

Of course, it is your right to disagree with Mr. Sundquist's position, as other Christians have. However, you have no right as a Christian to misrepresent James' position with such outward malice. Is your biblical defense of Rick Warren's teachings so weak that you have to resort to questioning James' character, instead of using Scripture to directly refute his criticisms against Warren?

Truly, your graceless condemnation of Sundquist is compounded by the fact that you hold him to a certain biblical standard of conduct (Matt. 18; Gal. 6) that apparently does not pertain to you. Sir, your hypocritical response has only brought condemnation upon yourself. Where is your gentleness in responding to Mr. Sundquist?

Do the right thing, Pastor: apologize for not reining in your tongue (Jam. 3) and resorting *ad hominem* against Mr. Sundquist. If you disagree with Mr. Sundquist's position and wish to refute it, then do so biblically. Attack his arguments if you will, but don't disparage his intentions or motives by implying he is a fool and a gossip. This is your biblical responsibility as a man of God.

Sincerely,
Chris Carmichael

Dear Pastor:

Please forgive me for correcting your mishandling of God's Word, but you are demonstrably mishandling it.

Matthew 18 is about going to a brother privately about his sin, not his false doctrine or public praxis. In Galatians Paul confronted Peter in the presence of all, and Rick Warren is no Peter. Your reasoning is not biblical reasoning, it is rather your own.

If something is published and circulated in the public domain, it cannot possibly be called gossip except by someone who does actually know what gossip is. A documented fact is not gossip, and documented facts by definition are not faulty.

If you are going to quote from 1 Corinthians you should quote from it in context (in Matthew 4 and Genesis 3 it is in the nature of Satan to cite God's Word out of context).

First Corinthians is a letter to be read comprehensively like any other letter. In chapter 1 Paul is warning against the sin of a party spirit by making a faction based on a personality cult where he appeals for no factions.

Further on in the same letter however in 1:19 where it comes to doctrine, Paul writes that there must be "factions" to prove which is true. The Greek term Paul uses for "factions" is *heraseis,* which means "heresy." God's Word says that heretical teaching is meant to cause division, and James Sundquist, Warren Smith, Dr. Larry Spargimino, and others have published fully documented proof that Rick Warren propagates heretical teaching. Such a man is not on our side, because he fundamentally contradicts God's Word.

If you wish to quote from Scripture, may I humbly suggest

you first try reading it in context. Secondly, kindly deal with the documented facts or don't deal at all.

Sincerely In Christ,
Jacob Prasch
Director
Moriel Ministries
www.moriel.org

Dear Pastor,

Your response is puzzling, to say the least.

Rather than respond in any cogent fashion to the charge that Rick Warren preaches many gospels among other things, it is easy to cast out veiled insults and cheap shots such as you have done. This does not require any thinking or study. In this vein, I would suggest you consider Proverbs 26:2,7,9. But of course, your work is precisely the work of the man in Proverbs 16:27.

I am sorry that you are so irritated by Mr. Sundquist's warnings concerning Rick Warren. No doubt Diotrephes also thought the same of John's warnings to the church of 3 John: SPAM, gossip, foolery, etc. Is your intellect so deficient that your only response is to cast firebrands at Mr. Sundquist?

To deal with fact and sound biblical teaching rather than distortions are Mr. Sundquist's concerns.

Accordingly, I am not surprised by your faulty use of Matthew 18. The context of this passage concerns personal sins of one brother against another. Rick Warren has not personally caused any offense to Mr. Sundquist but has, instead, taught and preached false doctrines and spread dangerous heresies most adequately demonstrated by Warren's essays in *Ladies Home Journal*, among other places. Mr. Warren's errors and heresies are very public and are to be dealt with as such—they are sins against God, not against any man.

Rick Warren has refused to respond to Mr. Sundquist (and others) who have brought to light his strange doctrines, especially his teachings on God's relationship to men in general. For that matter, you have not responded to nor defended the charge that Warren preaches other gospels.

Your further misuse of 1 Corinthians 1 is evidence that you lack a basic understanding of how Scripture is to be used. Suffice it to say, the admonitions in 1 Corinthians 1 are in regard to Christians following men—precisely what you seem to be doing. Warren and his followers are dividing the church by calling attention to themselves rather than to following Scripture carefully as we are commanded to do (1 Tim. 4:16). As some on the Internet blogs have suggested, it's "Pope Rick I." Rick Warren seems more intent on obtaining an obedient following than on preaching a single and simple gospel of repentance and faith in Christ. His distortions of key biblical words and terms must be brought to light, as Mr. Sundquist and others have bravely done—and bitterly opposed by the false shepherds such as yourself.

No—we do not consider you to be on "Jesus' team" but working instead for the Deceiver who is more intent on dividing the brothers and filling the church with tares—the unrepentant, in particular. You need to repent of following a man—Rick Warren—instead of the Jesus Christ of the Bible.

You should think carefully what "Jesus" it is that you preach.

Sincerely,
Hadley Robinson

About the Author

JAMES SUNDQUIST is the founder of Rock Salt Publishing, a biblical discernment ministry. He is the author of *Who's Driving the Purpose Driven Church?*, a documentary on the teachings of Rick Warren (available at www.swrc.com). He was the founder of another musical production company where he was the executive producer, composer, guitarist, and developer of health maintenance compliance software for such clients as Sony, NordicTrack, and *Prevention* magazine.

He wrote and produced two documentaries on the history of hymns and Christmas carols (for which James was nominated for a Grammy for Best Album Notes) aired on National Public Radio, Calvary Satellite Network, Family Life Radio Network, Salem Broadcasting, and the Armed Forces Radio Network. James' first solo record album is entitled *Freedom Flight*, on Lamb & Lion Records for Pat Boone Productions. He is also winner of the National Wilbur Award in broadcast journalism for his documentary on the history of hymns and won the Armstrong Memorial Research Foundation Certificated of Merit for his documentary on the history of Christmas carols.

James was also a biblical commentator with astronomer Dr. Danny Faulkner and Dr. Kent Hovind on a video creation series entitled: *Age of the Earth* for Creation Science Evangelism. He also wrote and produced a documentary and video on creation and prophecy, entitled: *Creation & Prophecy: Does God Expect Man To Be Able To Tell Time?*

James has been a guest on All Things Considered (National Public Radio), hundreds of Christian radio stations and national programs including Southwest Radio Ministries, VCY America, Radio Liberty, Andy Anderson Live (WMCA-WWDJ, New York), Drew Marshall Show (Toronto, Canada), Moody Broadcasting Network, Family Life Radio Network, The Byte Show, The Center for Changing Worldviews, The Edge with Daniel Ott, WMUZ Radio, and Creation Science Evangelism with Dr. Kent Hovind.

James is a regular contributor to a number of biblical discernment ministries and journals such as The Conservative Theological Journal, Worldview Weekend, Be Alert (Moriel), Despatch magazine (Australia), Christian Witness Ministries (Australia), Messianic Perspectives, Prophezine magazine, Former Catholics For Christ, Cutting Edge Ministries, Cephas Ministries, MacGregor Ministries; MM Outreach, Gentle Shepherd, Proclamation Invitation and Warning, Kjos Ministries, Apologetics Coordination Team, Apocalyptic Hope, The Midnight Herald, The Gist, Media Spotlight, Let Us Reason, Eastern Regional Watch, Spiritual Counterfeits Project, Prophecy Update—News & Information for the End Times, and Hope for the World. James has done research for Bob Dewaay on the purpose-driven and church growth movement and co-authored an article with him entitled: "How Rick Warren Is Masquerading as an Angel of Light Transforming Your Church and Country."

James also counsels families and churches in the U.S., Canada, Netherlands, New Zealand, Australia, Africa, and around the world who have been destroyed by purpose-driven teachings and programs.

Some of his articles and interviews may be accessed at *www.abrahamic-faith.com/False-Teachers.html*.